THREAD OF LIES

by

Myles Ojabo

DAFEL BOOKS

First published in 2020

Published by Dafel Books

(K and L publisher),

Auckland, New Zealand

ISBN 978-0473411770

Fiction

Other K & L Publications

Black River (2018) written by Myles Ojabo

K and L Anthology: Histories of Yesterday (2019) Edited by Myles Ojabo and Uchechukwu Umezurike

K and L Anthology: Black Dream, No Mask (2020) edited by Myles Ojabo

1.

The ceiling of the support home loomed above him as he walked into the building of white-painted walls. He sat on one of the brown leather sofas and waited. An airy sound echoed thrice through the building, a door slammed and the sound of the dragging footsteps of his brother Tito followed. Tito was in a night robe, his hairy chest exposed; he still maintained his unkempt beard. Sonny spotted Tito's bewildered countenance. When Sonny stood to shake hands, Tito's grip wasn't firm and he avoided looking into his brother's eyes.

Tito sat on a sofa opposite Sonny. 'Did you fly directly from Nigeria?'

'Had a long stopover in Qatar.' Sonny swallowed a gulp of air before he continued. 'I arrived New Zealand early this morning. How are you na?'

'You know I do not like to be asked that.'

Some silence lingered. 'Tito, I am concerned about you as much as Nina and Daddy and Mummy.'

'Bullshit. Bullshit, Sonny. How will you feel locked up in here?'

'Tito, you are here because you need help. You hear voices. You think weird things.'

'I do not need any goddamn help. Everyone hears voices. You have voices in your thoughts and your head.'

'Do you prefer to be locked up in jail back in Nigeria, or sent to those dysfunctional mental asylums in Lagos?'

'I am not supposed to be in here. I need freedom. Daddy or Mummy can help. Are they not part of the bloody government at home?'

'Tito . . .'

'Is the bloody government not in control of all the laws and policies?' Tito's eyes bore into Sonny's.

Sonny hated this argument. Forty-eight hours before his flight to Auckland, he attempted to reach Tito via phone. The first time, a staff said he could not speak to Tito unless there was permission from the boss of the support home. He spent thirty minutes on the phone to get approval. He waited six minutes more to speak to Tito.

'Hello.'

'Is that Tito?'

'I am sorry. Who do you say you are again?'

He felt sick saying his name one more time. 'I am Sonny, Tito's brother.'

'I am sorry. Tito cannot talk to you. Can you call back perhaps in an hour?'

'Can I speak to the other Nigerian-Australian who looks after Tito?'

'Michael is on leave, I am sorry.'

Sonny slammed down the phone.

An alarm went off. There was a shuffling of persons within the building. Tito laughed hysterically. Sonny saw good and evil in his eyes. He saw how Tito's death would bring grief to their family and wished his brother had a normal life. Memories from their teenage days returned to him. Nina, their only sister, had returned that evening from an extramural lesson. She walked into the living room and waved at Tito. He lost interest in the video game in front of him as Tito followed their sister into the bathroom. Sonny wondered if it happened again. When Tito returned to the living room, he looked distraught with water in his eyes. Their parents were out for the party of a Governor's son. The security guards chatted loudly outside.

'That bloody Ghanaian teacher touched her again . . . and she's bleeding.'

It nauseated Sonny once more. Nina's secrets tortured him and he hated to keep it and wished their parents knew. He took a gulp of their father's gin on the bookshelf; Tito drank twice as much; then they left home that night with three kitchen knives.

Both boys found the teacher's house in the grubby street that was flooded with rainwater. They kicked the door open and entered. They pounced on the forty-year-old Ghanaian teacher, kicked him and beat him with his plastic chairs. Tito struck him on his forehead with the hilt of the big kitchen knife. The assault went on. A kick from Tito sent the poor man to the floor. And Tito jabbed his knife into the man repeatedly, in the neck, chest and belly. Eight stabs, Sonny counted until the teacher's inanimate frame brought Sonny to a sudden stillness. He looked around – the windows were open – and shouted, 'Tito! Stop!' The effect of liquor earlier consumed had waned. They fled.

The teacher relied on breathing aid for months. Stitches covered his neck. The truth was never known; the Ghanaian feared the government and the father of his assailants. Years later, Sonny learnt that the teacher only mumbled the words 'armed robber' when questioned by the police.

'I would like to say thank you for informing the police about me,' Tito muttered, bringing Sonny back to the present. Sonny hated these words. Their mother used them against him severally. Nina too. Their father was the only one that gave him a thumbs-up for doing the right thing.

'You should be thanking me for this,' Sonny replied.

'Bloody hell. What are you saying?'

'You are here because you hear voices and will not give up your delusions, Tito.'

Tito stood and, breathing intensely, pointed a finger at Sonny. 'It is you, Daddy and Mummy who are mad, not me!'

Tito didn't attack him with punches but simply walked out of the lobby.

Sonny spoke to a staff about his interaction with Tito.

'Tito will get better,' the staff said.

Sonny sighed. 'But how? When?'

He left for the city afterwards in a rented car. He felt glad being away from Lagos or Warri traffic, where no one was in their right mind to give way or obey simple traffic rules. He needed to catch up with friends from his university days. Anton and Craig, the Kiwi brothers in his class at Portsmouth, England.

The Auckland winter felt like razor cuts on his body. Liquor would douse the cold and perhaps the tension of the time spent with Tito. Alcohol always linked his history to his dealings with Tito: the memory of another night back in Nigeria overcame him once more.

Sonny saw three policemen walk into the bar in the Nigerian town of Warri. His companions yelled at each other over a premiership game between Manchester United and Arsenal. He watched the policemen walk to the bartenders. There was a little conversation between them and the bartenders. Shortly after the policemen left, he lifted his fifth bottle of beer and approached one of the bartenders. He remembered his vision blurred and his speech garbled.

'They told us to turn down the music after we couldn't help them,' the bartender said. 'They asked if anyone walked in here in the past hour. We said you guys have been drinking here for three hours.'

'Who might they be looking for?' Sonny asked.

'They didn't say. But my second said the lesbian couple who live six or seven houses after a rubbish heap ahead were attacked.'

Sonny swayed his bottle repeatedly. He took a sip. The beer tasted bitter. He went back to his friends and called it a day.

They walked to the car parked under the mango tree. His friends doubted his composure and asked if he could drive. He ignored their questions, took the wheel and waited for them to make up their mind. They entered the car and he drove out.

He dropped off his friends and turned back in the direction he just came from, going further than the bar. He got to a house surrounded by smaller houses with brown, rusted zinc roofs. His greatest fear confronted him. The living room was disorganised, the cushions in disorderly arrangement. The centre table toppled against the wall and some of the framed pictures on the wall were broken on the floor.

'Lesbians and witches are all hated by God and should die!' Tito cried from his room.

Sonny opened the door to Tito's room.

'They are also humans, Tito,' Sonny's mother replied, in tears.

'Tell me the reason why God destroyed Sodom and Gomorrah.'

Tito was on the floor in tears; he clutched Nina's dress in one hand.

'I killed them! I killed them for God.'

Their father stood hands akimbo and had his usual look of tiredness.

The wardrobe in the wall looked rummaged and bashed in.

'We have been waiting for you, Sonny,' Nina said, quietly.

'Why? Why has no one called the police?' Sonny asked.

'No! No jail for me!' Tito went on.

Sonny took his phone out of his pocket.

* * *

In front of the bar on Beach Road in Auckland, his friends waited. Sonny hated to search for parking space but he soon found one. Drinking, to him, was truly one of life's superb ways of getting over his distress and unabated jetlag. He hated to pay for parking – that $7 parking fee could afford him an extra bottle of beer. In his part of Nigeria, touts collected parking fees from motorists. They claimed to own public spaces and terrorised people. The days before the killing of the lesbian couple in Nigeria came to mind, Sonny remembered the family in the dining room quietly eating rice and beef stew.

'Sodom will be destroyed again!' Tito lamented once more, which was his song all day.

'How the hell do we make him stop this, na?' Sonny asked Nina.

'Sodom wasn't a city of gay men and women. Go and learn to read your bible, Tito,' Nina said.

'You are wrong jor. I will help God destroy that world,' Tito said.

Sonny tried to douse the memory of the lame words he uttered that day. 'God needs the help of no man.'

As he shared the bedroom with Tito later that night, he endured another bizarre multiple personality disorder Tito launched into.

Tito pointed to a GPS application on his phone and said, 'Sonny, I can see where the lesbians are right now. Look, Sonny. See where that red spot is? It's a bar near the police barracks.'

'Tito, GPS does not work in Nigeria.'

'But mine works.'

Sonny longed for sleep but Tito wouldn't seal his lips.

2.

The traffic at night subsided early, which was unusual in Lagos. Michael Merije arrived at the bar an hour early and waited in a section lit by glow of red, blue and white bulbs. A slow music playing suited strong drinkers.

Rayleigh entered the bar and approached him. A slight agitation came on her face but she forced a smile and ran a finger through her hair. She raised her thinly carved brow when she sat and asked, 'Hope you don't mind if I smoke? It is nice to see you again.'

Her English accent didn't make her loud like the Brits he knew. 'I have been following the news about your sister's death,' Michael said.

'You weren't interested at first?'

'I had to get interested.'

'How old are you?' she asked.

'Thirty-three.'

Two women emerged from a door behind Rayleigh. They walked over to meet a chubby man at the counter.

'This country really amazes me. I offered bribe before I was allowed to look at police documents,' she said.

'I saw an article yesterday that links the deaths to the Niger Delta militants.'

'That's a lie.' She offered him a cigarette.

'I am sorry . . .'

'You want a drink, then? More drinks?'

'My belly already has enough beer for the night.'

'The beer here is really strong.'

'Yeah, easily puts one over a mountain,' he said, and watched her wave the bartender.

The bartender took her order and brought her drink.

'The government is hiding something. I will get to the truth. I owe my sister the truth.'

'Of course, you will find the truth.'

Rayleigh laughed. Her shoulders brushed Michael's as they walked out of the bar. She led him to her car, a red RAV4 parked yards away under a tree. He liked it. He wondered how she coped driving in Lagos. She leaned on the driver's door indolently, her body inviting him close to hers. He stared into her eyes. She suggested they take a walk.

'My driving would be terrible in this state,' she said, looking downwards, her hands on her waist.

He tried to recall if she finished the third bottle she bought; she hardly touched it. 'Can I drive you to your apartment?' he finally asked.

'I should be fine after a walk. There are many drunks behind the wheels in Lagos. It is fun. But isn't it funny?' she said, laughing. She placed her hand on his shoulder. 'I live in a hotel.'

Her excitement faded and she took her hands off his shoulder. She smiled sadly against the night. She wanted a break from the walk and found a suitable spot on a rock by the side of the road. It felt warm – a perfect spot to commune with the moon.

They lay with their backs on the rock and avoided each other's eyes. From the corner of his eyes, Michael saw the heaving of her breasts as she breathed.

'When I was a kid, I used to think the moon was Santa's home,' she said. 'My Dad told me Santa Claus was an angel.'

Michael gazed at her. 'I remember being told that, too.'

'I remember the Christmas mornings when Mum and Dad left Christmas presents in front of our bedroom doors and told me and my sister Kay that Santa came while we were asleep. It seems Kay always knew where the dolls, chocolates and lollies came from. She had been an atheist from an early age.' Rayleigh wiped the tears in her eyes. 'Do you love rocks?'

'I've never been really interested in landforms, but I love to spend time at the beach.'

'During most holidays as children, Mum and Dad usually sent Kay and me to Limerick where our great grandaunt Ivy lived. Her last husband was Irish. She brought Dad up when his parents passed away. Ivy took us to the beach where people said many children had died, but she told us we were protected. She told us our grandparents' spirits wouldn't let us die young, and let Kay and me swim in the rising waves to the amazement of other children monitored closely by their parents.'

'You shouldn't let these memories hurt you, Rayleigh. These are happy memories.'

'I am only crying because of . . . because . . . you fail to recognise how I feel,' she said, with a little laughter. Her stare held his briefly.

'Rayleigh,' he called, tilting her head with his hand. Her lips glistened with desire. 'Rayleigh, I am not into women.'

She opened her mouth as if to speak.

'I'm sorry but . . .'

'You don't have to say anything more,' she said.

* * *

My rigid parents left me with the impression that Nigeria was a spiritual place. I held on to another picture of Nigeria. War. My paternal grandfather was a known drunkard his village, Okigwe. He tapped good wine to sell. Sometimes he sold all the wine tapped, and on the days he couldn't sell, he came home drunk. He always sang a famous Igbo song about dying for Biafra when he was drunk.

'Your mates are at the war front dying for Biafra, and not singing,' my grandmother once challenged him.

'I am the best palm wine tapper in all of Okigwe, and if you do not understand the effect of palm wine, keep your mouth shut. Palm wine give fingers on triggers accuracy in the war. My wine is the best taken to the soldiers. And that's why we are going to win the war, or worse, die for Biafra,' my grandfather replied, his breath heavy with alcohol.

'Real men have been recruited and taken to fight. You are here dying for palm wine.' Grandmother never gave up.

Grandfather shut his ears to her words and sang his song about dying for Biafra louder.

When the Biafran troops in Enugu fell, the Nigerian Army advanced toward Okigwe. My old man, six then, remembered it well. Villagers ran and hid in a bunker dug beneath the house. Missiles came upon Okigwe like raindrops, tearing houses down. My father survived underneath the collapsed house he shared with his sisters. Grandmother and two of his sisters lost their lives underneath the same collapsed building.

Grandfather died while he was drunk with his Biafra song on his lips. He was on his way home that night. A missile hit him, smashing his ribs against the massive branches of a fallen tree.

Villagers found my father, a child then, underneath the debris of the house, rumpled zinc sheets and wrecked wood.

Memories of my parents visit me all the time as shame and betrayal. They were supposed to be the only ones I run to. But they stood against nature – my weakness – by rejecting who I am.

To my parents I must get married, except I desired the priesthood. 'If you cannot find a woman in Australia, I will go and find one in Nigeria for you,' my mother once said during a ride to the dairy where I got Dad a birthday present.

'I am tired of this verbal diarrhoea. Why can't you and Dad just leave me to deal with my personal life?'

'Do not forget your Christian upbringing.'

'Mum, can you tell me if Eve was Adam's partner or wife?'

'She was his wife.'

'Who wedded them?'

'God.'

'Mum, there is nowhere in the Bible that speaks of that.'

'What point are you trying to make?'

'I am open to any relationship for now and not marriage.'

'You need to see a psychiatrist. You are nuts and . . .'

'Mum, I said I am open to anyone at the moment, man or woman.'

The night became hard for her. She and Dad destroyed a few of my relationships.

'Why bring such disgrace to us?' Dad asked during the birthday barbeque.

'If it's disgrace, it's my name that sinks.'

'I have lived almost half of my life in Australia but I still know my roots. I still know where I

come from. Michael, you need to think. Know your values.'

'Who knows if it is a woman I might meet. I am open, Dad. I am.'

'Shame on you, Michael. Shame on me too. Shame on you, Edward,' Mum said, unable to look at Dad in the face. It had been a long time since she called Dad by his name.

When I was seeing my ex, Ash, he introduced me to magazines that showed naked men and women. My parents till this day blame him for the evil he planted in my life.

We were both fourteen. One time Ash and I explored the red light district on George Street. I picked a Chinese and a large Indian woman on the first night. Ash chose a slim blonde. We used a room that had two beds. I proved myself while Ash watched. I wanted his validation.

* * *

Rayleigh offered him a ride and he willingly accepted.

'Did you date girls?' she asked, fastening her seatbelt.

'I tried to but . . .'

'What?'

'I never felt I was in a relationship. They were no different from the girls I met in George Street. God forgive me, I cheated.'

'How many girls did you supposedly date?'

'Just two. I dated Annie for four months when I was fifteen. Then Orna, when I was seventeen, for nearly six months.'

'And the men you dated?'

'Quite a number of men. Ash. There was Paul – a Polynesian weightlifter who is now late. I met Okafor, a Nigerian, who was created out of lies; he broke me with his lies . . . I hate to talk about this.'

'Typical,' she said, shaking her head. She swerved onto Tokunbo lane and stopped by a bus stop beside a mosque. He saw that she was getting used to the unruly driving of the city.

'Many thanks, Rayleigh . . . and it was nice talking to you,' he said and stepped out of the car.

'Wait,' she said. He didn't catch what her eyes gave away. 'You didn't tell me the reason you are in Nigeria.'

'The reason . . .'

His mind wandered back to Pitt Street in Australia. He held a bottle in his hand, and marched in slow calculative steps, with slurs dripping from his mouth. He wanted to sing like his grandfather, to die for Biafra on Pitt Street. But who gave a damn about Biafra in Australia? He would die for being queer, hated for his sexuality by his family. He would never enjoy the relationships the straight people he knew had. He wanted more beer.

Another black man stood across the road preaching in an amplified voice. He condemned the street, pubs, prostitutes, homosexuals, burglars and rapists. Michael felt a connection to this man. He staggered across the road, not too mindful of the traffic. A driver shouted 'idiot' at him.

The black preacher ignored the abuses and apathy from passers-by and held his bible firmly above his head.

Michael watched and listened to the sermon about hell and paradise.

The preacher locked eyes with Michael and whispered in a tone different from his evangelising voice. 'Hey brother, you got a stronghold of unclean spirits around you.'

Michael felt the bottle in his hand drop.

'Brother, we need to talk. God loves you.'

They both entered a coffee shop a few yards from the Commonwealth Bank.

'How do I know you're a homosexual, brother?' the man, bald and probably in his early thirties, asked.

'I have no idea,' Michael replied.

'My name is Noble,' the man said. 'I am an anointed servant.'

They placed their orders.

'Where are you from, brother?'

Michael couldn't figure out the man's accent. 'Over here. I am from Sydney.'

'I mean where you got that black skin from.'

Michael spoke of his roots.

'I'm from Ghana,' the preacher said. 'Ghana and Nigeria are like Esau and Jacob. You will have to go back to Nigeria and deal with your problem. Your case is very complicated. I know many great men of God in Nigeria. I could give you the name of a church.'

It was pandemonium: the thundering of bare feet on concrete floor, fierce clapping of hands and nodding of heads, tongues yelling glossolalia, fire-filled languages and war songs against the camp of the devil. All this done on empty stomachs as the congregation was expected not to eat or drink for four days. Nigeria welcomed Michael this way.

The consistent shaking of his neck built muscles on his shoulders. His ears rang constantly. So much sweat. Body odours. Foul smell from people's mouths. His eyes always were widely opened, unlike the others that shut theirs tightly.

People openly submitted their issues to the leader of the congregation.

His condition was interpreted as a battle of the flesh. The spirit of lust supposedly lived in him. So he tried to kill his flesh to overcome evil. He prayed to kill a spirit man behind his problem. They asked him to place his palms over his groin.

Some women in search of fertility were asked to place hands on their wombs and pray.

Some men prayed fire against spirit women and enchantments in the atmosphere.

The first night, which he imagined was incredible, became a little scary. This side of God seemed entirely new. The second day he developed sore throat. He wondered if death awaited him on the third day. Well, he felt stronger. He believed he could do it - go on without food till the end. On the fourth day he was exhausted. He felt castrated. He couldn't remember if he fell asleep or fainted. In his unconscious state, he dreamt of a man chasing him. He turned around, yelled and swung a punch at the man in the dream. His chaser collapsed.

'After this fasting and waiting upon God's fight, you will realise a lot of changes, my son,' the counsellor assigned to him said, during one of their one-on-one meetings.

'I dreamt he died, the spirit man.'

'Good, good. You will soon start seeing the good things coming your way. You will have a beautiful wife who will have seven children for you. You'll also get a beautiful job in Australia. Mark my words.'

'Seven children? That's too much.'

The counsellor laughed. 'How many do you want?'

'Two or four would be alright.'

His counsellor, an attractive man whom he would love to take out for dinner, gave him hope and requested for an Australian suit. Michael promised to send him one when he was back in Australia.

He stood before the window in his hotel room and stared at the Atlantic Ocean, watching the waves play with themselves. Beside the need to fill his belly with food, he desired a drink. He needed cold, hard liquor. He needed to examine his heart, to test his body.

Two days after a four-day trial fast, he mounted a prostitute, a short woman of chocolate complexion and soft hips. When he was done, he lit his first cigarette in years. The woman slept deeply beside him. He fought the confusion in his head. He shoved aside the memories of his cleansing as he woke the woman.

'You have to go.'

'Can't I stay till the morning?'

'I'll be on my way out soon.'

She got up. Her nakedness his regret. She wore her clothes. He doubled her charge and handed her the naira notes. He went online using the computer in the room. It didn't take long to find a gay club and a map with directions. He called a taxi.

3.

Rayleigh's writing, which was a first love since her childhood, suffered after she graduated from East Anglia with a second class lower and found herself in journalism school two years later. Four months into a diploma degree, she signed a contract with London's 96.9 FM, where she did a midnight show. She sat at the reading table of her Lagos hotel room and scrolled through the condolence messages left by listeners on her Facebook page. *We love you, Ray. My heart is with you wherever you are. My partner and I can't wait for you to come back*. Rayleigh scrolled down quickly. She barely read the comments completely. *Whoever is behind the cruel murder of ya sister will surely face the axe. God bless you, honey. What sort of shit country is that? Do they also eat humans?*

She closed the Facebook page and created a new Microsoft Word document. As she stared at the screen her supervisor's painful comments on her creative project at East Anglia returned to her: 'The groundwork of Rayleigh Johnson's novel, especially the character development, is not realistic. Actions, dialogues, and sentence-level writing does not hold up to a standard I would expect at the master's level.' She had to write tonight anyway. About her sister's death and not do the head-throbbing documentary. She would get into the head of her sister's lover. She would start with the first person point of view and even try out the second person point of view her supervisor indicated she was weak with.

I stand before your grave this day to say I knew you better after you left. You were brought up under structures that see same-sex relationships as sinful. Yet you embraced your nature in the face of persecution.

I want to say I am sorry for taking the feelings you shared with your lover for granted. I want to say I am sorry for keeping you away. I was insane. I am still in a deep search for reconciliation and the meaning of fate and death.

You never expected to turn out a lesbian until you turned fifteen. Before then, you were still a virgin, keeping yourself for a destined husband. You were unlike my sister who had her first experience at thirteen. Did you ever have a picture of an ideal man ever in your life? Tall, nice whiskers, well-built?

I knew Sayo was your first lover from the first page of the diary you kept in '96. You met her two days after your fifteenth birthday when you joined the choir at Saint Mary's. She had a boyish figure? You would never forget the evening she invited you for dinner at her place in Akoka. Your parents were okay with it since she wasn't a boy. How old was she? Twenty-three, I reckon. And after a lovely dinner, you described her approach as rape, was it? She was rough and her fingers burned like fire. They were also damp, from touching that secret place between your thighs. You were excited, but afraid. You were more excited than in your wet dreams.

While you walked home that night, I guess you recalled the guilt that held you captive, the religious upbringing, the bondage your parents had around you. Three more times in the same week, it occurred. And the first Saturday after that first starry-eyed night, the confessional stood against the real person you would become.

'Bless me father for I have sinned, my last confession was two – sorry, three weeks ago,' you said, after kneeling in front of the confessional.

Father Ubong blessed you with the sign of the cross and asked, 'What are your sins, dear one?'

'I for . . . for . . . fornicated. I fornicated with a . . . with a . . .'

'It's alright. You don't need to mention who he is. You should know that Jesus loves us all the time. Whenever you have sex with a man who is not your husband and then ask for God's forgiveness you crucify Christ all over again.' After a sigh, he asked. 'What other sins do you have to confess?'

'I lied to my parents, and I lost my temper and raised my voice against my brother.'

'Parents are the most precious gifts any child in the world can have. We live in a world where so many kids are orphaned or born out of wedlock. You should not treat your parents carelessly, daughter. You should also seek for the Virgin Mary's direction in handling your anger. Say the "Hail Mary" fifteen times, "The Lord's Prayer" seven times. Now, say the "Act of Contrition".'

Your struggle continued. Sayo's curvy hips wouldn't fade from your mind; neither would the love of God.

The next day was a Sunday. It wrecked you and you gave in to the lustful glances at unremitting intervals between you and Sayo in the choir section. The glances carried the weight of your first lovemaking, and you could not adjust to the tempo that the choir members sang – A Cry Against Goliath. You didn't receive the Holy Communion. But Sayo did.

Mass ended. You felt controlled, pulled, drawn helplessly to her. You smiled and laughed, walking beside her on that road toward Pako bus stop. Two of you took the right turn just before the roundabout ahead, heading to the street she lived. A yellow bus with black stripes bumped into another bus in front of it. Two of you laughed as one of the drivers alighted and rushed at the other still behind the wheel. You wanted Sayo more than she wanted you. Inside the house with the door shut, she drew you into her arms, and you hungrily licked the tongue she stuck into your mouth. You let her hands clasp your breasts. She undressed you, gently pulling down the zip behind you. She pushed you against the bed that took up most of the space in the room. Your lips trembled. Your body trembled. You were afraid to moan, fearing the walls. You tried to give voice to your confused conscience.

'This is immoral, Sayo,' you said, breathing hard.

Sayo sat up in bed and gave you a mean stare. 'Why now, Ejiro? Why did you not see it as a sin before we did it?'

'Because I couldn't control myself. You brought me into this.'

'We are matured enough to determine what is right, Ejiro. We are not married, neither do we have boyfriends that satisfy these desires. I do not have a thing for boys and I see the same in you. We just have to remain in this till one day, maybe, true husbands shall come.'

'I am not comfortable. Virgin Mary, help me.'

The arguments kept growing. You were in front of the confessional again – after three weeks.

'I had sex with a fellow girl.'

The priest remained in silence. This silence squeezed your throat. Father Ubong prayed for your soul, sprinkling holy water on you like you needed a bath of it.

For penance, he asked you to recite the entire rosary three times. He advised you to keep a scapular around your neck and sin no more. Anger possessed your body on the way home.

You headed toward Pako bus stop. Traffic was bad. You arrived at Sayo's place but met her absence. You sat on her doorstep, pulled off the scapular and waited. Night came. Your parents expected you home before nightfall but you didn't care. Sayo finally returned. You couldn't wait for Sayo to settle. You devoured her, to her surprise, just after she opened the door and both of you entered the house. You pressed and licked her breasts. You drew up her dress above her waist. She spread legs. You touched her. Her moans dared the neighbours to do their worst. Were you doing this to hurt God or Father Ubong? While she kissed your neck, you caught the sight of the scapular lying on the floor just before the door.

The pesky words of your parents waited for you at home. As you got tougher their words became useless, unable to leave a scratch on you. You stopped going to confession. You told yourself God wasn't deaf and started relying on personal confessions. You knew Sayo better; she was tight-fisted and careless. She neglected your company each time Manchester United played. She loved the company of men, not for sex, but for the love of squabbling. She argued in the bar a few hundred metres away from where she lived with whoever wasn't a United fan.

She introduced you to wild parties. One time, both of you were past inebriation. She caressed you on the dance floor. This sparked a gossip; in the church, other choir members avoided both of you.

You hated arguments so you gave in each time something went wrong between you two, like the time she accused you of staring at Sylvester, a boy in the choir. She didn't like you for giving up too easily. She hated your quietness in public. She wanted you to be like her. To challenge men as she did.

You dreamt of yourself mothering a baby. You woke up one day crying like a child, and wept asking the Virgin Mary for help. Your mother heard you and knocked on your door. You wanted to be left alone. You developed a hard skin. You pulled out of the choir and started to avoid Sayo. One Saturday, you saw her at the entrance of the market. You turned around, as though you forgot something, and headed back home.

A week later, you failed to see her in the same market. She confronted you.

'That demonic thing we do has to stop, Sayo.'

'Ejiro, it is not easy. It would have been better if it hadn't started at all.'

'So?'

'It's not just the desires. We have both failed to recognise our love.'

Those words dragged you into what you never imagined possible to accept. You fought against the opening of your heart. You became more confused, and for weeks you did nothing vital than to sit and think. You were lucky the holiday from school had just started. You experienced many sleepless nights. You eventually stopped going to church but you couldn't stop thinking about Sayo.

Rayleigh minimised the Word document page and opened the horrible PDF file of the project report that troubled her for many nights. She found a paragraph and read it aloud and wondered: 'However, Rayleigh Johnson's creative writing suffers from a lack of focus on issues rather than characters, there are a number of characters in her work, but they tend too often to be caricatures, stereotypes, one-dimensional. That is, the novel is intent on showing the suffering that characters endure, but . . .' She stopped. Shook her head and thought of how she wouldn't create a stereotypical Ejiro, a caricature Ejiro. She closed her eyes . . .

Your aunt pushed you to join a Pentecostal Church when your parents cried over your acquired habit of staying home on Sundays. In one service, amid the congregation's thundering of feet and speaking in tongues, the pastor pointed at you. Your heart raced. You didn't want him to tell the church you were a lesbian. You saw him cast out demons from people in previous services.

'God is taking you to a foreign land,' he said.

You felt relieved. You didn't think of the prophetic words until you reached home. Your affection for the church increased. Many Nigerians desired to go overseas. You wanted to leave Nigeria. You wanted to forget Sayo, but within your heart, you still missed her.

The words in your diary say that whenever you missed her like this she showed up. She came to your house. You told your siblings to tell her you were not home. But Sayo waited all day and this made your parents worried.

Your mother entered your room to ask why you didn't want to see Sayo.

'I realised she wasn't a good person,' you told her.

Your mother managed to convince Sayo to leave. You started to stay away from home. You joined the cleaners department of the new church and this took most of your time until school resumed. Just before you turned seventeen, your parents gathered some money to send you abroad for undergraduate studies. The pastor's words were true. You left the shores of Lagos to study English Literature in Britain. This became the final disconnection from Sayo's world; the news hit her like a rock. You received numerous letters from her in your first year. The scar you left her never healed. She claimed to shove her body beneath various men in search of love.

You made friends at the university in London. You became part of an Indian family that let one of their rooms to you. You fell in love with schooling. Your religious devotion became bounteous in a recommended Pentecostal church. Classmates called you 'Radical Lady', after you challenged Kay Johnson for presuming Jesus loved gay people in his lifetime.

'How can such a worthless remark be spoken about God?'

Her silence didn't satisfy you. You nearly slapped her. You wished you spat on her.

Months later, she surprised you by offering an apology. Her smile quenched the anger you possessed against her.

Rayleigh lost hold of the story; the tapping sound of her fingers on the keyboard distracted her; she could not visualise Ejiro anymore, couldn't imagine her sister sitting in the same classroom with Ejiro. She stood up and walked to the side of the door, turned off the light and walked to her bed.

4.

Michael deleted the two emails sent to him by his father.

A chat message popped up on his screen.

Rayleigh: Hello there. Why aren't you in bed yet?

Michael: Just couldn't sleep. Perhaps thinking about you.

Rayleigh: Liar!

Michael: Did you speak to Tito's sister?

Rayleigh: I did. She is lovable.

Michael: (Sighs) . . . and helpful?

Rayleigh: I just wrote a piece she inspired. I tried to get into her head in a way. I hope I got it right.

Michael: What do you mean?

Rayleigh: I wrote something, a short story.

Michael: I will like to read it. It's good to know you have picked up the pen again.

Rayleigh: Words live in me, even though my one-time supervisor back in the day thought otherwise. I can let you read it.

Michael: Please, put it through.

An email with an attachment file of the short story she'd written entered Michael's inbox. He opened it and scrolled through to see the length before he began reading:

My parents wanted a girl after having two boys. My grandmother foresaw my birth and assured my father he would have a daughter. My father named me after his mother. Nina Oghentega Ogheneovo. We grew up as happy kids. I never knew my elder brother, Tito, suffered from any mental issue. He appeared clever and normal to me. Daddy and Mummy did everything to please him, and I wondered why they had to.

I hold memories of our primary school days. One break time, I stood in front of Primary 2A, Tito's class, and watched him. He sat among some boys who enjoyed listening to his tales. He saw me and left the crowd around him. He knew when I wanted part of his lunch. He knew when something went wrong.

Tito asked, 'Who is looking for your trouble?'

I only nodded my head, so he could follow me and see. A bully in my class dared to call me a skinny grasshopper.

The bully saw us and sprinted out of the class through the doorway to the football field; and Tito chased after him.

The next term I sat in the same class with Tito. The bully became his disciple and followed Tito about. Tito's notoriety made me a queen in my class. In the next term, I was sad to leave him behind. I do not know how to describe the feeling. I was just a little girl. I overheard Daddy say to the headmaster – Tito had brain problems. The bully moved on too and stopped being Tito's disciple.

My eldest brother, Sonny, wasn't like Tito. He didn't play soccer, for which Tito was popular. Only a few of our friends in school knew him to be our elder brother. He was quiet and, I bet, ashamed of Tito and me. I knew his mates constantly bullied him. Many times, he covered his head on the desk and cried. It was what Julie, a girl in his class, told me. But Sonny swore in the name of heaven and earth and denied ever crying.

The three of us only united outside the school premises, particularly when we were alone at birthday parties and picnics. My brothers were my rock. They beat up boys that called me their wife. There were times when I felt lonely, when Tito and Sonny became so attached to their video game at home, so that if I asked to play, they claimed games weren't for girls. The same thing happened whenever they watched football. They both supported Arsenal. I liked Manchester United because Daddy owned a Manchester United jersey. They told me to shut up each time I predicted a Ruud van Nistelrooy goal. I always stood alone except on the days Daddy was home.

I had a special attachment to Tito until I got into Primary 4. I went on an hour's visit to see our neighbours who shared a fence with us. The visit turned out to be the last of all my visits there. Kagiso, the only child of the family, was a few months older than me. I heard something I wasn't supposed to hear. Her father, South Africa's new envoy in Nigeria, saw me off to the gate.

I sighted more policemen on duty under the palm tree by the corner of our house. Daddy and Mummy's convoy of cars littered the premises. The eyes of the policemen all fell on me. 'Good day, small madam,' one of them greeted. I heard Daddy's laughter within the house.

I entered the house through the back door that led to the children's lounge. The house help, with a mop in hand, looked up.

'Have you seen my brothers?' I asked.

'They should be in the garden.'

I recalled they had a week to transplant some flowers from a nursery bed into a set of flowerpots Mummy brought home. I found them there, squatted, hands stained with soil. Tito searched my eyes.

'I don't think I will ever go to Kagiso's house again. I heard their mother telling a woman some bad things about Daddy,' I said.

'What did she say?' Tito asked.

'Don't believe her, Tito. I guess Kagiso refused to give her that mug of ice-cream today,' Sonny said.

'You open your big mouth at home, but at school, you are as dumb as a lizard.'

Sonny fetched some sand with his hands to throw at me. Tito shielded me. The sand hit him on the back.

I wanted to scream and urge Tito to fight Sonny. Tito held my hands tight and asked, 'What did Kagiso's mother say?'

'She told the other woman that Daddy was a criminal,' I said.

Sonny drew closer.

'She said Daddy was among the politicians taking away Nigeria's oil to sell in South Africa. She said Daddy built companies in India but couldn't build any here in Nigeria. She said she had been telling Kagiso's father to stop Kagiso from seeing me. Kagiso and I were listening with our ears on the door.'

'And what did Kagiso say?'

'She said her mother was a bad woman but asked me not to tell anyone. It pained me to hear all that.'

'We should teach them a lesson,' Tito suggested.

'That's not my business,' Sonny said. He turned on the tap in the garden, washed his hands and left.

Tito sat on the ground matted with grass. The shadows of the trees fought against the sunlight and pulled in a breeze. The leaves swayed. I sat next to him.

'Their cat will pay for all she said. Titan will pay,' Tito said.

I smiled. The South Africans loved Titan the cat. Unfortunately, the cat jumped over the fence every evening into our garden to find food. I loved feeding her. Sonny loved her, too. Tito never did; I imagined him torment the animal. I was ready to give the animal a bang on the head. We waited. The moon appeared in the sky. One of the policemen came into the garden to see if we were okay.

Titan soon jumped over the fence. She was light brownish in colour and blind in one eye. Kagiso said a car had run over her in the past. A veterinarian, their mother would never forget, kept Titan alive. She survived on milk from a toddler's bottle for months. I now wanted to discourage Tito from the intended harm. He whispered the cat's name, offering an empty hand. Tito grabbed her to my horror.

'What are you going to do, Tito?'

He ignored me. I approached him and patted Titan. The cat yelled. Tito's grip became firmer.

'Let her go,' I said.

'We should rip it apart,' he replied.

A chill overcame me. I stepped backward, turned around and ran out of the garden.

I paced in my room. I failed to imagine Tito's action. I ran to the store opposite the kitchen and climbed on a bench to look through the window. Tito held a pair of scissors in his hand. Titan struggled and wiggled her tail. My heart ached. Blood spattered against Tito's face. I lost my footing and fell. I cried.

I ran in front of the house. Tito and Sonny were with Daddy. Tito looked away. He had changed his shirt. Sonny mistakenly dropped some keys to the floor. I ran into Daddy's embrace in tears.

'What is it, Nina?' Daddy asked.

I drew my face backward, turned and pointed at Tito. 'He killed Titan.'

Daddy looked into my eyes. 'Are you sure?'

I nodded.

Daddy looked at Tito.

Sonny's face drooped.

'Tito, did you?'

'I did it because Kagiso's mother called you a criminal.'

Daddy stared back at me. 'Nina, you must not speak about this to anyone, especially Kagiso. Do you understand?'

I nodded my head.

Daddy walked toward Tito. 'Show me what you did,' he said.

Tito led Daddy to the garden.

Michael: (after nodding, he minimised the Word document and clicked on his chat icon) Still up?

Rayleigh: Yep. Done?

Michael: So sad. Knowing Tito, the story is very plausible.

Rayleigh: Did the narrator sound Nigerian?

Michael: I think so.

5.

The plane glided in the clouds and descended on the runway of Murtala Mohammed airport. Rayleigh sighed. She failed to hold back her tears. The Lebanese man who sat beside her offered her his handkerchief. The plane slowed to a smooth stop and the exit door opened. Passengers impatiently pulled their hand luggage from the overhead compartment and crowded the aisle. Rayleigh cleaned her face and remained in her seat. An Indian woman, knocked over by a Nigerian woman, yelled in Hindi.

Rayleigh met Chioma in one of the lobby. Chioma appeared plumper and wore longer hair. They embraced.

'Welcome to Nigeria. Nice trip?'

'Gosh! I cannot complain.'

Chioma saw the tears in Rayleigh's eyes and embraced Rayleigh for the second time. 'I understand. Let me get your luggage.'

'I need to be in Warri.'

'Of course, it's a fifteen minute flight. It won't take long before we get to the local airport.'

Rayleigh sweated as anticipated, having followed the weather updates. She smelled the dust in the air. They soon found a taxi.

* * *

She entered the ladies' room at the local airport and wept into a flannel Chioma offered her.

'You mean, Blaack Afrrica?' she stressed as she replied her late sister, Kay, when she made up her mind about Nigeria.

'Come on Ray, I know you have this thing against Africa, but it is a continent our forebears lived for,' Kay replied, folding a pair of jeans into her luggage.

'Our great grandparents were Christians. Missionaries, Kay, don't kid me. You have never been to church,' Rayleigh said, and sprawled on a couch in the Neasden apartment Kay shared with Ejiro.

'We want Nigeria. Ejiro and I want Nigeria. We have made up our minds. And, please, it disgusts me when you call Africa that way.'

The past brought more tears to her eyes. Rayleigh took her seat in a smaller plane. Chioma sat beside her. It was silence, tears, sighs, regrets, and confusion throughout the flight.

The plane landed in Warri. Both women pushed their way through the crowd. Chioma stopped in front of two soldiers. They nodded. Rayleigh led Chioma a few yards away from the men.

'You should have told me.'

'I knew you would object,' Chioma replied.

'I should feel comfortable. I am not in Hitler's Germany.'

'Are you sure your feelings say the same things? In Lagos, no problem. But this is Warri,' Chioma replied.

The soldiers tailed them.

She stood in front of the window and saw the soldiers in their back and forth movement within the premises. Their guns hung from their backs with the nozzles pointed upward.

The trees provided a shade for the small garden Kay nurtured. Rayleigh found her way down to the lounge using the stairs Kay and Ejiro walked on numerous times. The lounge looked tidy as if there hadn't been death in the house. She stood in front of the kitchen wooden door that mocked her. Rayleigh fought the urge to walk into the kitchen where Kay and Ejiro were murdered. She walked out of the house and met Chioma who sat on a chair reading a novel.

'What do you think?' Rayleigh asked with tears in her eyes.

'You need strength, Rayleigh'

A repetitive nuisance caught Chioma's ears. 'What's that?' She slanted her head to listen. The noise came from a crowd: *Kill am! Kill am! Kill am!* Screams. Cries. Hysteric laughter.

A naked man ran past the entrance to Kay's compound and a crowd armed with stones, sticks and machetes chased after him. The voices of the mob soon faded. The two soldiers with Rayleigh and Chioma walked to the entrance, and after a brief discussion, one of them followed the mob. The soldier who stayed back and continued pacing.

'It's common for a whole street to chase a thief who was caught stealing,' Chioma said. 'If the soldier does not get involved in time, the thief dies by jungle justice. People put tyres over the unlucky thief and set him ablaze.'

Rayleigh froze. 'For stealing?'

'Yes, for stealing petty things like a purse or a watch.' Chioma rubbed her chin

'People do forty to sixty hours of community service for stealing little things like that in England. How come they spared Tito?'

Silence.

Rayleigh remembered the Jurgens twins. On a bus ride from London to Neasden, she'd begun a conversation with the passenger who sat beside her.

'I wish you had black hair,' Peter said.

She tried not to be offended by his remark. 'Kay, my twin, has blonde hair,' she said.

He revealed to her he had a twin brother, too.

'We could meet – the four of us – for a drink.'

A week later, Rayleigh arrived at Kay's apartment with the twin brothers in a loud old 1967 Cadillac Deville they claimed their granddad left them. She jumped out of the car. 'I will be back with her,' she said and ran to the house in her colourful shorts.

Rayleigh entered the house and met Kay in a conversation with Ejiro.

'Why aren't you ready, Kay?'

'I am not going anywhere. I changed my mind.'

'Don't bloody tell me that.'

Ejiro didn't raise her head. Kay stood up, took Rayleigh's arm and led her to the kitchen.

'Stop putting up an attitude each time you find Ejiro here. It isn't cool. I have always told you to treat people equally. She isn't a stool or a wall. She has feelings. You make her fear you. She feels bad and won't say it, but I know.'

You told me you were having a break from your affair with her and I was trying to hook you with Sol.'

'Of course I wanted a break. But I didn't tell you I wanted my heart to be toyed with. You became the happiest woman in Britain when I told you I was having problems with Ejiro, and now you are trying to hook me up with Sol. I never told you what happened with the last dude you introduced to me. I will say it to your face now! Brian broke me! He drugged me, paid a hooker to make love to me while he watched with his friends.'

'That cannot be true.'

'Ask him and tell me whatever he says. I want you to give me and Ejiro some time to sort things out.'

Rayleigh went back to Peter and Sol. Their stereo sounded louder. She forced a smile even though she felt like killing someone and told them Kay had company.

6.

Rayleigh walked into the bar to speak to her producer about the interview she needed to do. She was so disorganised and still undecided about using the local camera crew recommended by Darryl, since hers was yet to arrive in Lagos. A man with dreadlocks approached their table, apologised for prying on their discussion and told them he was a skilled cameraman with no job. He made her laugh in her distress over the last couple of unproductive weeks. She persuaded Darryl to hire him.

The next day, they were on their way to Ejiro's parent's house. Michael, who anticipated a nightmare to occur during the visit, joined them. Darryl believed it would be fine.

She wasn't bold enough to knock, so Michael did. It took a few seconds before a woman, obviously Ejiro's mother, opened the door. She smiled at Michael and Darryl but frowned at Rayleigh. She ushered them in, led them through the sitting room that smelled of dust. They walked past a set of brown sofas. The standing fan by the corner produced an irritating sound as it spun at a snail's pace. They sat in the dining.

Darryl placed his Samsung notebook on the table.

'What can I do for you?' the woman asked.

'Well, I am Rayleigh Johnson, Kay's sister.'

'I think I know who you are,' she interrupted Rayleigh. 'Please, you will excuse me. I need to let my husband know of this visit.'

'If this isn't a proper time, we can come later,' Michael said.

'No, no. It is in our culture that a woman must let her husband know of every visitor that comes to the house,' she said, and left.

Silence took the woman's place.

'We should go,' Rayleigh whispered.

Darryl smiled.

They heard the angry voice of a man somewhere in the house. Michael reached for Rayleigh's fidgety fingers on the table.

Ejiro's father, middle-aged, stout and bald, appeared in a pair of knickers and a white singlet with several torn spots. He narrowed his eyes at the visitors.

'Have you all come to kill us?' he asked quietly, at first. 'Isn't my daughter's blood enough for you?' His eyes settled on Rayleigh.

Rayleigh wanted to be on her feet. Michael held her back. The man's wife reached for her husband's shoulder. She spoke to him in Urhobo.

Her husband held Rayleigh's gaze as he listened. Then he looked at Darryl and pushed his wife away gently. He confronted Darryl and grabbed Darryl's neck. The table screeched. The chairs fell. Michael and Rayleigh found their feet. Rayleigh shut her eyes briefly as the man's wife screamed. Ejiro's father took Darryl's notebook in one hand and held onto Darryl with his other hand. He flung the notebook against the wall. It split in two.

Darryl struggled, trying to push him away.

Michael approached them and pulled Darryl away from the man's hold.

'Sir, we understand your anger. But you also have to understand that we bear the same loss. Your daughter died. That woman standing there,' Michael pointed, 'also lost her sister. We did not kill any of them. All we are doing is searching for peace and truth.'

'What justice can be done when she has already been killed because of you foreigners and your lifestyle? My daughter died many years before she was murdered because of the repugnant lifestyle she adopted,' he shouted.

Darryl stared at the pieces of his notebook.

'Can we sit down and talk?' Michael asked.

The man nodded.

Ejiro's mother rearranged the chairs.

Ejiro's father sat down and rested his chin on his palm. Michael motioned at Rayleigh. He wanted her to say something but Rayleigh wondered what she could say. The little drama had stolen whatever words belonged to her. The visit was a mistake. The soft-spoken woman, sitting beside her husband, let out a cry.

'We have been pretending everything is behind us. Truth is, we are still trying to put everything behind us. And you all come here to reopen our wounds. What have I done to God to deserve this? Why? Why? Why?'

Ejiro's father hissed.

Michael stared at Rayleigh. She stared back at him, and then stared at the woman. 'I am sorry,' she said.

Suddenly, they heard someone's movement outside the front door. This was followed by a grunt. The woman's voice ceased. The door opened. A man in his thirties entered the house. 'What is going on here?' he demanded.

'She has come with no trouble. She's the sister of the white girl . . . of Ejiro's white girlfriend,' Ejiro's father said.

He was certainly Ejiro's brother, because he dashed for Rayleigh. Rayleigh stood up. Frozen. Michael took a stand in front of her.

He stared into Michael's eyes and asked, 'How can a woman have sex with a woman? Explain?'

'She is her sister,' Michael said. 'She's just Kay's sister.'

Rayleigh moved from Michael's back.

Ejiro's brother took a step backward, squatted, then rose and jabbed his head into Michael's belly. Rayleigh screamed; someone took hold of her right hand. She looked at her side and saw Darryl, who pulled her, heading for the door. 'We need to get out of here!' Darryl screamed.

Rayleigh turned around and saw Michael flung on the floor. He managed to rise and evaded the punch aimed at his face.

Darryl pulled her outside and they ran. Rayleigh did not stop to look back. She slipped and fell into a pool of mud. Darryl, a yard in front, ran back and helped her up. He slipped and fell too. She heard him laugh. When she looked back, she saw Michael limping toward them.

7.

Michael hated being judged for including Tito in the team. 'They will accuse me of bias, since we are both black,' he once said. On this glorious moment, Tito's dream came true. Before now, the team displayed weakness, eighty-eight minutes of play and nothing to show other than three off-target shots. The Ashby team scored early and his teammates, lacking zeal, began to kick the ball out of the pitch at every opportunity. Michael, an acting coach for Tito's house, was furious.

Michael asked Tito to get ready to jump on to the pitch with just six minutes left to play. Tito waited for this day. He had the name 'Tito' instead of his surname 'Ogheneovo' above the jersey number 18. He jogged in. The booing from the spectators increased. *What the hell is wrong with coach Michael? Who the hell is the black retard? A black retarded coach sending in another clueless retarded idiot.*

Since Michael gave no instructions, Tito attacked from the left flank, even with the pressure still hard against his team. Bleddyn's magic paved the way – a pass that came with reluctance from outside his eighteen-yard box in guided accuracy. He trapped the ball and within the last three minutes of the match, he dribbled his way through the opposing players, and from the mid-field he aimed for the net and shot the ball. The goalkeeper couldn't reach the goalpost before the ball hit the net. Tito fell on your knees in tears. His teammates surrounded him and knelt like he did. 'You are the king, man!' Bleddyn screamed in his ears.

'You are the true king,' another teammate said. 'You are the king! King!'

With five minutes of extra time added, and with two minutes already taken away, Tito celebrated with his teammates blithely. Every player on the pitch wanted to settle for a draw, but he continued to chase the ball using his last energy.

In the last minute, an Ashby defender indecisively passed the ball to his goalkeeper who passed it back to him. Tito charged against the defender who slipped and fell, and so Tito had the ball. Supporters held their breath in feverish adrenaline and he sent the ball into the net with the velocity of demons. The keeper failed to stop the ball. A hush took over him in a split second. He fell to his knees and felt the grass again as his teammates surrounded him. The whistle shrilled.

Michael shook his hand and Bleddyn patted him on the back.

'That shouldn't get into your head,' Dwain, who didn't shake Tito's hand, said.

'Don't listen to him,' Bleddyn whispered into Tito's ear.

'Cap, I know what you are telling him, but that's the fact,' Dwain said. 'He has a lot to learn.'

'Leave him alone for now, Dwain,' Bleddyn replied, dragging Tito away.

Tito recalled the day police brought Dwain to Rangatahi House; how it became known that Dwain was a child molester who put marijuana in his little daughters' food in Whangarei. He still believed marijuana cured mental disorder.

Medication was given to patients in the evening and most of them wanted access to their rooms.

'What does it feel like rescuing the team today from what could have been a disastrous defeat,' Bleddyn, pretending to be pressman, asked.

'I wouldn't say I saved the team. God did it,' Tito replied.

'Next test for us is against Totara House. What do you foresee?'

'We can only do our best.'

'Thank you so much, Tito. I wish you luck in the future.'

'Thanks.'

'You should request a phone call to your family to tell them about the day,' Bleddyn said.

Tito shook his head and told Bleddyn how his father never supported his passion for soccer; how he thought Sonny and Nina were the ones with great futures.

Bleddyn looked around. The staff were in the office. He slipped something into Tito's hands. Tito looked around.

'You are in safe hands, Tito,' Bleddyn added.

'Weed?' Tito asked.

'My sister sneaked it to me during her last visit.'

'We can meet at night when the bloody night staff are all asleep. I can teach you how to create fire from the socket in your room. Just leave your room door slightly open.'

Bleddyn had been in Mason for about six years. He was half Maori but had lived with his white mother most of his life. His assaults on his mother started in his late teenage years. She reported his third attack, after he had stabbed her by the side of her belly. Tito often heard him chat to himself and laugh out loudly in his room during the night.

Tito couldn't sleep and waited in anticipation. Once it was past midnight, he snuck out, tapped on Bleddyn's door, and went back to his room. Bleddyn came into his room a few minutes later. He pulled out two thin wires from the socket using a pen. The sparkle from the wires lit Tito's roll of marijuana. He dragged the contagious fumes and enjoyed the sensation in his body. Soon, he lost any sense of awareness. When Bleddyn asked Tito to think of a past girlfriend, he did it enthusiastically. He thought of Ngozi, his cousin in Nigeria. Her photo, which he kept, was of her large breasts and a heavy backside. He remained still while Bleddyn's palms caressed his hips and the sides of his stomach. Tito adjusted himself, easing it for Bleddyn to pull off his pants. The realisation that he was naked and aroused made Tito laugh. His body trembled as Bleddyn got rid of his underwear, forcing Ngozi's breasts and backside out of his head. He willed his body to sustain the arousal he felt. And Bleddyn's thrusts and body thrashed over him, tracing Tito's lips and spine with his fingers, Tito's thighs and neck. All over.

* * *

'You gay!' said Ejiro and Kay, the women he murdered in Nigeria.

'No, I'm not,' Tito replied.

'Yes, you are. Kill yourself,' the women said in unison.

He woke up but their voices remained in his head.

'You seem to have grown a tail,' Ejiro's voice said. He heard the white woman laugh.

'I got no tail,' he said in rebuttal even though he felt something behind him.

The women's voices faded. His room smelled of Bleddyn. He couldn't remember what transpired after he was high on the weed. He wore some clean clothes and pressed the call button in the room. A staff came and he told him he felt something strange in his body. Perhaps a tail. He fought the pictures trying to force themselves into his mind.

'Where,' the staff asked.

'In my bum,' he said.

'Come with me,' the staff said, and led him through the main lobby to the clinic. He called for the assistance of a second staff.

'Pull your pants down and lie on the bed.'

Tito did so.

'I can't see nothing. You bullshitting,' the staff said.

'Why will I do that?' he replied.

'We will go see the doctor later today,' the staff concluded.

Two staff members escorted him to the Bruce McLaren medical centre in the afternoon. A British doctor said the same thing. Nothing was wrong. 'I can't even send you for screening.'

Tito went training in the evening. Michael asked him to wait on the sideline. He watched the others receive instructions and undergo drills. He yawned.

Bleddyn jogged toward Tito, his eyes looking over his shoulders first, before they met his gaze.

'Why late?'

'Felt sick and had to see the doctor,' Tito replied. 'What happened last night?'

'We got so high. Still trying to get the feeling off the shoulders.'

'What did you do to me?'

'Did you fantasise about me, mate?'

Michael called Bleddyn and he ran off. Tito remembered some scenes from last night and felt like bashing his head on a wall. Michael called Tito twice before he looked up.

* * *

His mother had flown in from Nigeria. But he didn't want to see her. She kept calling the support home while he was in the soccer field. He was informed by a staff that she had booked an appointment to visit the following day. She came with a grey-haired African man who looked very thin in an old brown suit. He had facial marks, thick scars on both cheeks. Tito didn't want his mother's embrace but she pulled him into her arms.

'This is Pastor Akagwu,' his mother said, introducing the scarified man in the old brown suit.

'Did you come with him from Nigeria?' he asked.

'No. He pastors a church here in Auckland.'

'What happened to Pastor Kunle,' he asked.

'Tito, we know Pastor Kunle is the reason you ended up here. You kept hearing his voice in your head to go after those women. God bless their souls. This is a different pastor.'

He looked at the pastor.

'Tito, you would be great in this life if I pray deliverance upon your life,' the man said.

'This is insane, Mummy,' he said, looking at her. 'I know – I know I'm sick in the head, but I'm right on this one. This man with you is also insane.'

'Stop that, son,' she said, glancing at the pastor. 'Tito, there is something very important we have come to talk to you about other than my visit.'

'I'm listening, Mummy.'

The pastor cleared his throat. 'Tito,' he started. 'You are not sick in the head. You are possessed by strange spirits. You will have to let me pray for you. I was on the pulpit last Sunday and I had a revelation. You are heading to the grave if you aren't delivered from these strange spirits.'

'Mummy, this is bullshit. This man here needs a mental health assessment. Such shit?'

'Tito, you need to listen. Don't talk about a man of God like this.'

'My ears are filled. I may hear voices, but I certainly know I'm not possessed.'

'You can't understand the things of the spirit,' the pastor said.

He didn't let them pray for him. He refused the garri and plantain chips his mother brought for him. He couldn't sleep at night, trembling at every slight movement of the curtain. In the morning, his head felt light. The invisible tail began to gnaw his butt again.

Bleddyn kept his distance from him.

He jogged onto the training ground and a ball hit his face. The ball, thrown by teammate Blake, bounced off. Blake crowed like a cock as Tito massaged the painful area of his face hit by the ball. A few teammates laughed.

Tito ran several times from one goalpost to another. He chased the ball within a circle formed by five teammates. They passed the ball amongst themselves to ensure he didn't get it. On the sideline, Bleddyn, with a foot over a ball, stood beside Blake and three others. He spoke looking in Tito's direction, and this weakened Tito.

Tito finally got the ball from Rodriguez. A smile of mockery settled on his face. Instead of the feeling of triumph, he felt loss. The laughter directed at him from Bleddyn and his company hit him like a spear. Dwain made a monkey face at Tito. Coach Michael, standing in midfield, ignored the boys' attitudes and continued his conversation with the goalkeepers. Tito wondered if the tail behind sprouted out visibly? He squatted, supporting his head with his hands.

'Hey. Get up, Tito. Show us your ass,' Dwain shouted. Bleddyn laughed, and it dug up a buried scene in Tito's heart. Bleddyn's thrusts, breaths, moans, and saliva. The sheets. The room. Tito got up and ran toward the other boys. Their laughter faded.

He aimed for Bleddyn's right cheek and raised a fist. Dwain caught his hand. Bleddyn stepped back. Dwain twisted Tito's arm and pushed him to the ground.

'Hold it Blackanese,' Dwain said.

Michael hit his alarm. Other staff ran into the pitch and surrounded Tito. He stood up and didn't say a word.

Later in the evening, he confronted Bleddyn in the main lobby of the building. 'You saying shit about me,' Tito said.

'This is New Zealand, Tito. Gay people are free.'

'Who the hell is gay?' Tito barked.

'Are you going to ask me to come to your room tonight?' Bleddyn asked.

'You goddamn swine.'

Bleddyn laughed. 'Do I look like a swine?'

When he retired to his room after supper, he hit his forehead against the wall repeatedly until blood dripped.

* * *

Tito spat on the grass on an important day there was a game against Kauri House. He was proud of his Number 18 jersey.

The match began.

Tito kept reassuring himself that no tail sprouted from his arse. There were superb passes at first from the midfield but they became scarce. The day turned out agonizingly boring. The ball avoided him. He ran about in aimless abandon. He tried to plant himself in vital positions. The midfielders Bleddyn and Mike were up to this. Kauri House supporters cheered their team. Tito felt the hideous tail; it felt so real that he sat on the grass despairingly as the referee blew the whistle. The referee, a casual staff, approached to see if Tito was injured. 'I'm okay,' Tito said, got up and jogged to the midfield. The spirits of the lesbians and the grey-haired pastor who visited with his mother entered his imagination. Bleddyn scored an own goal five minutes before the half-time whistle. Kauri House players patted each other on the back and their supporters cheered.

None of Tito's teammates complained about Bleddyn's ridiculous attempt to give away a corner kick, which became an own goal. Michael only talked about Tito's absence in the game and demanded more from him. He wanted Tito to fall back a little and help in the midfield.

Back on the pitch, Tito became overly eager to tackle the opposition. It paid off in the seventy-fifth minute when Michael got to his feet. Tito tackled the opposition's goalkeeper, won the ball and ran past a Kauri House defender. Kauri House supporters went quiet. He shot the ball.

Bleddyn approached Tito and patted his back. Michael kicked the air. His fears fell into his fists. Tito thought to himself, what did he just do? He shot the ball over the goalpost!

'Even a chicken could score that!' he heard Michael say.

Tito ran to him, gathered the bitter taste in his mouth and spat at Michael's face. Michael swore. Tito swore back and took two steps toward Michael, and an alarm went off. A number of staff surrounded them. Tito was held down, pinned to the ground.

'He will never play again,' Michael said.

The next morning, Duncan the house manager came to see Tito, and they sat in one of the meeting rooms.

'Hey, shithead, you need to behave well if you want to remain in this place. We are considering transferring you to a more restrictive unit.'

'I'm sorry, Duncan.'

'You have to apologise to Michael. How can you do that to your country man?'

Tito apologised during training the next day but Michael ignored him. His involvement with the team was uncertain.

Training ended and he walked up to Michael again and said, 'I said I am sorry!'

Michael looked up, licked his lips and said, 'I hold nothing against you. I do not hold grudges. I forgot about the incident the moment I left the pitch. You just have to know that whatever you do works for or against you. But I must warn you to never try that again!'

* * *

Dwain started to avoid Tito. Bleddyn only spoke to Tito when he saw the need to correct Tito's tactics. During the training, Tito glided against Bleddyn's foot. The alarm buzzed. Bleddyn remained down for nearly half an hour attended by some nurses. Tito felt glad about this. Michael's eyes wouldn't leave Tito: *what were you thinking when you charged at him?* But Tito only wished he could do the same thing to Dwain. Michael ended the training after Bleddyn was taken to the clinic. Tito's peers went back to the support home with a sense of loss.

Tito told Michael he was sorry again and Michael replied the same way as the last time. He didn't hold grudges outside the pitch.

Bleddyn's injury worsened and he couldn't play in the year's tournament anymore.

Tito was on the bench when his team faced Rata House. They lost. He asked Michael to his face if he knew what he was doing.

* * *

The hospital discharged Bleddyn and a nurse returned him to the home. Tito saw Bleddyn's bandaged leg and desired to kick it. He was going to inflict Bleddyn with the grief in his heart. He blamed Bleddyn for his relegation in the football team. Bleddyn's eyes met Tito's.

'Damn homo!' Bleddyn muttered.

'Cut that crap,' the nurse behind Bleddyn's wheelchair said.

This angered Tito. He snatched a crutch leaning on the wall, raised it over his head and let it fall on Bleddyn's bad leg.

Bleddyn flinched.

The nurse attempted to press her alarm.

'If you do that, I will pick up the crutch and use it on you,' Tito threatened the nurse. He stared at Bleddyn and continued, 'You think I do not know what you and the other players say behind my back? You pretended to be my pal. As a kid, I enjoyed cutting frogs and lizards up. I enjoyed seeing puppies dying under car tyres. I enjoyed tearing up cats.' He raised the crutch up again. This time he hit it hard against Bleddyn's right shoulder.

Bleddyn groaned and fell to the floor.

The nurse, scared to raise her voice, shivered.

Tito squatted before Bleddyn and looked into his eyes. 'You really think that I am gay? I see the way you look at me.' Tito stood and climbed onto Bleddyn's bandaged leg. The nurse looked away. Bleddyn kicked. He held one of the cushions tightly. The nurse hit the alarm and some staff around rushed onto the scene.

Tito desired to kick the breath out of Bleddyn. Instead, he sank to the floor and began crying. 'What is wrong with me?' he lamented, his hands sprawled over his head. 'What is wrong with me?'

8.

The Kiribati culture was almost dead when my son Paul left the Island. Although the festivals were still celebrated and we felt our ancestors' breath among us.

Paul left for Australia to become a professional weightlifter and I thanked my ancestors for his success. He sent me clothes, money and books about Australia, unlike his siblings who only sent me infestations, nightmares and toothaches from the stone-throw distances they had built their huts.

Five years after he left the Island, some white men, who said they were scientists, came and prophesied evil upon the land. Many Kiribatians, including me, rebuked their prophecies and asked the scientists to leave.

'The priest is saying the same thing. The sea will devour the land soon,' my wife said to me.

'What does your religion know, woman?'

'The demons you still worship are the problems,' she replied.

I laughed. 'Have you ever seen your God? Who is this unknown God, by the way?'

She left the bedroom that night.

Enele, my cousin, shared some of my beliefs. He was one of the few people who was happy about my son's success in Australia. But he didn't accept my son's sexuality. He said Paul infuriated our ancestors.

'Will your father in the ancestral realm be proud of Paul?' Enele asked me.

'What are you talking about? What concerns my father what his grandson does in private? If I decide to bury my sperm in the soil, it's nobody's business.'

Shortly after the rainy season started, it came to pass that the evil words of white men shocked the Island. Overnight, a powerful wind from the sea swept a part of the Island. Later in the day, I received an invitation to be part of a meeting of the village elders. We discussed nothing but paced aimlessly, scrutinising the shores; and at the end, suggested stupid remedies for the wreckage of wind's onslaught the night before. We reassured ourselves that our ancestors were not asleep and refused to link the tragedy to the predictions of the scientists.

It dawned on us a few days later that we were wrong. News came that neighbouring Islands had been devastated, too. Our fears increased. In unsettled times like this, what should one mourn? I kept myself busy fishing during most of the days.

On a particular day while fishing with my youngest children, we saw the true devastation of the island.

'That's where Ma Joseph's house used to be.' My youngest child Alika pointed.

'No. That was where we used to go and watch the cultural dance,' Anitelu said.

Two years separated them. On our way back home, we came across angry and frightened men and women. Their greetings came at me like spears.

'Our ancestors are not asleep.' I tried to give them hope.

'What ancestors? The ones rotting in hell for their idolatry?' one of the Christians among them replied.

What could I say? I blamed the white man. We wouldn't have been trampling on our religions.

So one day, I went fishing and injured my finger with my hook. I couldn't fish anymore and returned to the shore where I met Enele and two elders waiting. They cornered me under a tree away from other fishermen and gave me the news.

I slumped, my knees dug into the soil, and I cried.

'It is the will of our ancestors,' one of the elders said.

'What will?' I asked. 'Why should a son die before his father?'

'You shouldn't question our ancestors,' Enele replied.

I pressed my palms against my face. Enele and the two elders accompanied me home where members of my wife's church already gathered and sang hymns. My grown children scattered around the island were around. My wife chose a pig for the night.

Days later, I spoke to Paul's next of kin. People said he was the one whom Paul buried his sperm in. They said he was an Australian black man and he was black like our first ancestors. But on the phone, this man spoke through his nose like a white man.

Enele eyed me as I fidgeted with the phone. He wanted me to accuse the man on the other end over Paul's death; all I wanted was Paul's body returned home.

'Much cheaper to have him buried in Sydney,' Paul's man suggested.

'Sell his houses, his cars, his jewellery, everything in his name. Use the money to send me his body.'

It took a week for him to arrive with Paul in a coffin. There were many threats for him from my people. But no one threw a stone at him because his perfume possessed charms. He was tall, slim and calm, and had a striking look. He wore a laurel made of grass over his shoulders like we all did. He held tears in his eyes but did not cry as we did.

We opened the coffin. My son's beard had a pinch of grey that was absent the last time he visited me. He still possessed our look. I stared at him with tears on my cheeks. How did cancer get hold of you, I wanted to ask. Did you smoke, or was it the thing you had with this man? My other children in attendance paid their respects. Paul's lover paid his, too, attracting scorn. He placed his lips on Paul's forehead. The gravediggers standing by impatiently stared as sand dripped off their shovels.

Two weeks after the burial, another terrible storm hit the island. It rained for two days and a flood washed over the entire island. Our anxiety increased. I bit my lips at Paul's grave submerged in water. One night I could sleep; I saw myself in Australia, far away from my culture, losing communion with my ancestors. I worked as a gardener for two women married to each other. They paid me well in Australian dollars. I smiled in my sleep. Then I woke up. I didn't want to leave my land.

'You and your demons will rot in this land,' my wife said to me, when I announced nothing would make me leave.

'And you and your children will someday die and then live forever in heaven, I guess. I will be glad to be like that rich man in hell who could see Lazarus in heaven. At least I will be able to still stare at your hips,' I replied, trying to touch the loosened knot of her lappa.

She slapped off my hand. 'If you do not make up your mind about leaving in three days, I will leave with my children. I hope you are listening?'

'I would die seventeen times here,' I said.

She said nothing.

The white men came again with their blackboards to explain the reason why we needed to evacuate. How could I leave?

My wife made up her mind and left me and my island, which she mocked my ancestors could not save. I waited for the water to return and eat up the land I grew up in and it did. Paul's grave. My farmland. My house. Everything. My wife and my children got into the boat; Enele and his family, too. I watched many other boys, girls, women and men get into the boat. To the nearest safe island.

'Papa, when will you join us?' Alika asked.

'Soon, my boy, soon,' I replied.

Anitelu waved. My wife's retrained the tears in her eyes. She didn't wave. She hated my loyalty to my homeland and my ancestors.

We were few that remained. Three days after the boats departed with so many Kiribatians, a rain that wouldn't stop started. Days passed. A week. Salt infested our drinkable water. The ocean flowed into the village and found channels into houses. It rushed into mine, where I lived alone, and rose up to my knees. Houses around mine collapsed. Roofs fell in. Walls fell. Decomposing flora floated on water.

9.

She tamed the desire to smoke and lay quietly on her bed. It was her sixth attempt to give up on her search for the truth since Kay's death. As her eyes wilfully closed, she fell into a nightmare where a giant gorilla chased her. Each stamp of the gorilla's feet raised the wind and she fell several times as she ran from it. She turned around quickly to catch a glimpse of the dark, hairy monster and saw its ghoulish eyes and chalk-white teeth clenched. She screamed and jolted awake, breathing intensely. She called reception and placed an order for a pack of cigarettes; it was 4.30 am; the cigarettes soon arrived. She went to the balcony, sat on a rocking chair and ended her two weeks of being clean of tobacco. It was going to be a silly day.

* * *

Rayleigh hated Darryl's shrewdness and over-confidence; she didn't like the way he blinked when she complained to him that the woman playing Kay's role wasn't the right choice, which he insisted was perfect and sensuous, as the imagination of what lesbian models looked like.

Lynda did not look like her sister. *Kay wasn't romantic. Kay wasn't big in her chest.* Lynda had a Welsh accent, she's was too thin, and walked like a man. This wasn't her sister. But Darryl was a respected filmmaker.

'I have been in this business for more than twenty years and I am giving up my career if she doesn't turn out terrific.'

'Darryl, this is not a film about lesbians. This is about my life. It's about my reconciliation with Kay. It's about my search for the truth. It isn't about history, or about making money. This means a lot to me.'

'And you think I would dump my Germany project and come to Nigeria for something that is worthless?' he replied. He put his hands in his pockets and squinted. His spectacles were spotless – just like his polished shoes.

'You are a woman of high taste. Pretty, determined and focused. You are like me, Ray. I don't why like-minded people find it hard to work together.'

Rayleigh glanced at the cameras standing yards to her left. She would tell him to his face at the end of the day that his cameras were outdated. The funding for the film was worth *The Sound of Music*. For now silence stood between them; she hated him and his neat, beardless face; and she hated the floor he stood on. He insisted on a house that was nothing like her sister's as the setting. She wanted the setting in Warri, where the clouds were darker. Darryl chose Lagos. She said the film wasn't fiction; he said the project was a depiction of true events; she was sick of him.

Repeatedly, the Welsh woman fell to the floor in false pains. Chukwudi, the slender man playing Tito, stood with legs apart, destroying not just flesh but the entire scene. He was passionate. The fake blood used on Kay's actor made the body messy. The character of Ejiro was played well. Rayleigh pictured Kay's distant and eccentric stare and her voice, between compunction and undertones.

'Look at her. Tell me she doesn't play Kay well,' Darryl said.

'She's got nothing, but . . . but . . .'

'But what?' he asked and lit a cigarette.

She didn't reply. She accepted his cigarette and lit it.

'The best of the shooting should be done at night,' Darryl said. 'The weather might be cooler then.'

But her sister's blood had to flow under the bright sun.

'Rayleigh, this is about perfect picture, good acting and terrific images. If I were to make a movie about my boring childhood, I would take the scene of my father's death when he slipped and hit his head on a gravel floor, and make it look as if he slipped and hit his head on the sharp edge of a rock. I would do this to reveal more pain for the audience to feel it.'

Rayleigh blew smoke rings into the air. Their oval shapes were no different from the bullying truth in Darryl's words. She blew some more smoke, this time, harder.

Later in the evening, she stood between two cameramen and watched the Welsh woman embody her sister's life and death as the actress fall to the floor with a moan, as Tito's club bludgeoned her repeatedly. For the first time in hours, she saw an incarnation of Tito in Chukwudi; the mien and anger she searched for.

She did not let Darryl know he had gotten it right. Tears filled her eyes. She opened her purse and brought out her shades, which she put on to shield her tears. *This time, Tito drags Ejiro out of the basement. He uses the club again. Blood splatters. Ejiro rolls on the floor.*

'Damn lesbians. Dumber than animals! Dumber than animals! Tito laments. He squats, still bludgeoning Ejiro with the club. 'Even a she-goat knows a he-goat!'

Rayleigh listened to Ejiro's moans, rising above Kay's. *Ejiro acts contrary to Darryl's instructions but he doesn't scream 'Cut!'*

Rayleigh looked away.

What happened to the guitar, Kay? The one granddad thought would take you around the world. The guitar you used to win the hearts of school kids in South London. What happened to the music? What happened to the dream of having children?

Rayleigh also thought about the un-replied emails. Not the ones she wrote Kay. The ones she wrote Ejiro whom she called names. Witch, bitch, whore, beast, murderer. No replies. How she accused Ejiro of causing her grandma's death. Her grandma died earlier than she had to, worrying over Kay living in Africa. Kay had only sent flowers and was absent at the funeral.

'I hated her for taking my sister away. For four years, I did not see my sister. Not until now, did I realise what my sister really shared with her. Beyond their relationship, they were more than sisters. Ejiro was more of a sister to Kay than I was.'

Rayleigh read the lines three times; she felt they gave away too much. Darryl collected the sheets.

She sat. He read the lines, stopped, and asked, 'What is wrong with this?'

'I don't like them.'

'You wrote them.'

'I will work on it.'

The sheets fell to his side, over a table. He rested a leg on the bench next to her seat. She smelt the garlic and tobacco on his breath. 'A journalist brings out the bomb in the story first – in the headlines, to catch the attention of viewers or readers. And what happens to the rest of the story? It becomes a recount. A novelist makes a real story. Bores you off with a first chapter, takes you on an interesting journey, reveals secrets, creates clues, and the bomb goes off at the end. Rayleigh, you have both of these qualities.'

He walked way. She stared at the sheets, and then looked away and saw Chukwudi, with a club in hand, climb the steps to the house. She took the sheets from the table and widened her eyes in reluctance.

It takes a strong psychoactive agent to make people do the things they do in the name of religion. I witnessed in Pakistan in my days of covering flashpoints around the world, a young boy of sixteen, handsome and strong, scream to the greatness of his God, blow himself and a dozen others up.

She liked the paragraph. It would introduce the scene where she found the support home managing Tito. She remembered as she gazed at Tito and Michael when she saw them the first time.

As I sat in front of them, I felt rage boiling inside me. . . . Suddenly, I knew what it felt like to be a big cat, a tiger, confined in the zoo. All those silly humans, taunting you from outside. I knew I wanted to rip them to shreds. I wanted to growl, to rip this killer to shreds. He sat there, avoiding my eyes. He knew me, I don't know how. Kay and I don't look alike. I was blonde, Kay wasn't. But he recognised me. Perhaps it was guilt causing his agitation. I wanted to devour him. Trapped in my flesh, I wished he attacked me under the guise of mental illness.

His eyes searched my body. The clock ticked. For a moment, I felt a bomb would explode. But I felt a kind of satisfaction beyond explanation. I was able to look into the eyes of the man who killed my sister.

Rayleigh got up. Her eyes met Darryl's, who was talking to Chukwudi. He came back to her.

'What's the problem, Rayleigh? You are scaring me!' He collected the sheets. A smile came to his face. 'I should give you a kiss for this. This speaks about the future without you knowing it. Rayleigh, I understand your emotions toward the project. I am lying if I tell you that you aren't distracting me. If you could go back to your hotel and put your head on a pillow for a while, it would be very helpful to me and the crew, and even to you.'

As she walked home on the dusty road, she came upon a group of children who stared and laughed at her. One little girl with her matted dreads raised a ditty that made them convulse with laughter:

Oyibo pepper
If you eati pepper
You go yellow more more.

The tallest among them gave the singer a knock and then shouted in Rayleigh's direction, 'Good evening, ma.'

A motorcycle sped past her on the darkening street brightened by security lights. The rider and his passenger looked back. This startled her. In her hotel, she sat on the bed and rested her elbows on her thighs. On her desk was a draft of her work in progress, a composite novel which Michael, Tito and Kay were major influences. Rayleigh remembered Michael questions about the work a few days ago.

'I am anxious to know what you are writing about me, anyway. What is a composite novel?'

'There are still arguments amongst literary scholars on what a composite novel is, Michael. My intention is to write a novel in which each chapter of the work can stand as a short story of its own. Some scholars have called works like this a Short Story Cycle. Some even argue it is a Short Story Composite.'

'I am a drongo; I need to really get educated.'

She didn't want to think of Michael. Her eyes settled on the sheets of papers and remembered the Friday night that changed everything. She met a guy who she didn't know was a minor and had a go with him. They got drunk together. He was shy on the dance floor and was reluctant as they walked to her apartment. She dragged Owen in and tried to be a different person. Their shadows over the wall entangled as they kissed.

They hadn't slept for an hour when the landline rang. Owen sat up. She switched on the light. Her nudity embarrassed him.

'Who the hell is this?' she said.

It was a female voice.

'Can you say that again?'

'It's me, Chioma.'

'Oh!'

'Rayleigh, I understand it's odd to call now . . . but it concerns your sister.'

Rayleigh tried to stitch the torn nerves in her head. Did Chioma run into Kay and her whore partner?

'Your sister was attacked. It's terrible, Rayleigh.'

'What . . . what happened? Who attacked her?'

'We do not know yet.'

'Where is she now?'

Silence.

The whore had killed her sister.

'Is she dead, Chioma?'

'I am . . . It's critical. You need to come to Nigeria.' Chioma's voice broke.

Rayleigh sensed Owen's movement behind her. She swallowed the tartness of alcohol in her mouth.

'Are you still there, Rayleigh?'

'I will get back to you. I hope I can reach you . . .' she got the phone off her ear, looked at the screen, and turned on the phone speaker. 'I hope I can reach you through this number?'

'Yes. It's my mobile.'

She hung up. Owen tried to touch her.

'Get your filthy hands off me!'

He trembled.

She didn't look at him but sensed his awkwardness in the way he leaped from the bed.

'If there is . . .'

'You have nothing to offer right now besides getting out of here!'

He put on his shoes, sorted out his vest and jacket among her clothes. 'Sorry . . . I am sorry,' he muttered.

Her eyes remained on the door after he had left.

10.

I was Tito's assigned guardian. He was a twenty-three year old patient and Nigerian like me. His parents in Nigeria were eminent people in the government. I arrived in New Zealand from Australia less than a year ago to be away from my parents. I worked sixty hours a week and had to send money to Okafor in Singapore. I had rent to pay. I was thirty-three but felt a bit older.

In the support home, we supported the mentally ill. Most of them were rescued from the street; some, under court orders for committing crimes. We gave them a life.

I became Tito's best guardian and he wanted me as his close acquaintance most of the time. But there were times I was absent on annual leave, touring the South Island. There were times I caught a flu and called in sick. Tito could jump over the fence and head for the motorway if he didn't like the staff assigned to him.

The manager, Phiona Gardner, thought it was inappropriate for a Nigerian-Kiwi patient to be supported by a Nigerian-Australian. She transferred me to Kahurangi House in South Auckland. Pacifica staff supported Pacifica patients in this same mental health service.

Maori staff supported Maori patients and Indian staff supported Indian patients. My case was different.

Phiona was a thorn in my side. It wasn't long ago that she reduced my wages, demoting me to level two. She said I lacked qualification. The former regional manager wasn't dumb to have it that way. He knew my worth. Tito got me back from Onehunga. He sprawled on a sofa in the lounge and brought out his penis in front of three staff. The only female staff among them sighed and went out. Tito laughed and kneaded his prick, calling her name. Two patients in the lobby took interest in this. They giggled and watched curiously.

Tito had no record of masturbating in public. Days, and weeks, went by. He faced the consequence of his behaviour. He was grounded – and he hated to miss his weekly outings. So he became arrant; he smeared the bathroom walls with faeces, swore it wasn't him and lied it was Archibald and Ethan.

Kahurangi House was different. I was assigned to Kelvin Milner and Arana Etera. Kelvin, a thirty-three year old from Wellington, had a mind of a seven year old. Respectful, adding 'thank you' to any request he made –

'Michael, can you get me some juice? Thank you.' He played with toys and made his bed neatly every morning. He rearranged anything that went out of place. I thought Arana was more difficult to work with until one Saturday morning, Kelvin lifted the fifty-two inch television in the lobby and threw it on the floor.

I always had my eyes, like a hawk, on fourteen-year-old Arana whenever we went out. Public toilets were his favourite spaces. When a staff once took his eyes off him for a minute while they were out in a park, Arana disappeared. He was found watching a five-year-old girl pee in the ladies' room. The girl's father left a scar on his chin and the staff was fired.

* * *

I was last to be informed about the meeting because Phiona never wanted me around. I had no doubt she, like Arana, had something against Africans. Against Tito. Against me.

'Why does no one want to work with Tito? I want to know!' she demanded, narrowing her eyes. And she was attractive.

'I never avoid Tito,' I quietly said.

She ignored me and creased her forehead, hoping someone else would speak. 'Well, I am considering writing to Tito's parents and their lawyer about his stay with us,' she said. 'If he is difficult to handle, we cannot keep him.'

'I see no reason for that, when we have a suitable staff that can keep him in good space,' Victor, one of the care managers, said. 'I am talking about Michael. I came back from my annual leave and heard Michael had been transferred. It shocked me. It shouldn't surprise anyone that Tito is playing up. For chrissake, we all know Tito behaves well when Michael is around.'

Phiona stared at the papers in front of her. She tapped her fingers on the desk continuously, brushed her hair aside, and then lifted her pen and made a note.

I was transferred back. The other staff failed to water the flowers we groomed indoors in the lounge. The leaves were pale and the stems and stalks were frail. The soil in the flowerpots had hardened. Tito brought me a red bowl filled to the brim with water. I watered the plants. He helped me transport them to the terrace, where they would catch the light from the sun.

It didn't take long before I got into trouble.

I had never been carried away by any woman's beauty since making up my mind about my sexuality. It was when we met Rayleigh. At the mall where I went with Tito to get him some new clothes. I guessed she was in her mid-thirties, and so tall a woman, with wide hips. She had a pair of blue jeans and a grey sleeveless top with green stripes. Surprisingly, she walked up to us.

'Rayleigh,' she said, offering a handshake.

'Michael,' I said.

Tito looked away.

She bought us coffee at a café. Tito dragged his feet and I am sure she noticed.

'Isn't she such a beauty?' I whispered to him. I held his hand and he pulled away.

'Cappuccino?'

'Yes, please,' I replied.

We all sat. I let the paper bag holding Tito's clothes fall beside my legs. Tito placed his hands above his head and covered his ears. He nodded sideways when I touched him. Later on, he fidgeted with his room keys and looked at her once.

'I guess you are English,' I said looking at her.

'Isn't it obvious?' she replied.

Tito uttered no word. She said it was nice meeting us and left me her number. Tito was quiet throughout our drive back. I reflected, hoping I didn't reveal any information about him. 'Have you met Rayleigh before?'

'No.'

'She looks nice.'

'Please, leave me alone.'

Tito kicked the door on his side open before I stopped the car.

'Hey Tito, hold it.'

'What?'

'Don't be a pain in the arse,' I raised my voice.

He hesitated, with one of his legs already out of the car.

'I don't want you saying anything to anyone about the woman we met. Do you understand?'

'Yes, I do.'

'If you say anything to anyone, I will lose my job and you will never see me again. Hope you understand me well?'

'I do.'

In the lobby I felt hot. One of the staff, Singh, had the gas heater on – and kept all the windows closed. I wondered how the other patients and staff watched the television in such an oppressive atmosphere. Tito headed straight for the passage that led to his room. We heard the slamming of his door. Singh and the others stared at me as I opened a window. Tito hadn't run into the house showing off his new clothes as he normally did.

I knocked on Tito's door an hour later.

'Go away. I do not want to talk to anyone,' he shouted.

He came out at dinnertime and ate a little portion of rice with more sauce than he needed. He ate silently at the table. One of the patients said Tito's father had called from Nigeria while we were out. Tito didn't say a word. Singh wanted to know if the food tasted too spicy but Tito ignored him.

In Tito's progress report, I wrote:

13:30 – 20:00: Tito had lunch with two other patients at 13:30. He had toast and coffee. One of the staff (Singh) reminded him about his scheduled shopping. Tito was rude to him. He told him to mind his business and I cautioned him, reminding him that he always had to respect people.

Tito got ready for his shopping at 16:00. He insisted to take the front seat even after I asked him to sit in the back of the van.

At the mall, he picked two shirts and a pair of jeans. He wouldn't pay for a paper bag, which nearly resulted in an incident. I showed him a notice that said paper bags must be paid for. He paid after this.

Back in the house at 19:00, Tito spent a little time in his room before coming out to have dinner. He added a lot of sauce to his rice. He ignored another patient, Frankie, who told him his father had called from Nigeria. He also ignored Singh who asked him if the food was too spicy.

I drove home that night troubled. I tried to visualise Rayleigh in my heart; her blush, her smile; I remembered how she walked to the café.

I woke up with a headache the next morning. The phone was ringing. My shift was an afternoon one. I threw off the duvet and answered the phone. It was Phiona.

'You do not have to resume your shift today. Just report here at the CBD office.' She sounded excited.

I went into the bathroom and stared at the shower. I spilled part my toothpaste over the sink before getting it on my toothbrush. I washed my face and put on a green polo shirt over a pair of jeans, and then wore my sneakers.

Tito, who sat among the management team, pretended not to notice me when I walked into the office.

'Let's start,' Phiona said.

Tito's eyes avoided mine.

'Have a seat, Michael,' said Phiona.

I sat. Mohammed, who took over from me last night, also avoided looking in my direction. My most recent right-hand man, Victor, rubbed his chin and listened.

'Tito, can you repeat everything you told Mohammed after Michael left yesterday?' Phiona began.

'. . I do not want Michael to look after me anymore. He does not do things properly as he did before. Yesterday, he met a woman at the mall just after we finished shopping and didn't give me much attention. He told me she was beautiful and he couldn't stop staring at her. The woman invited us for some coffee, which he accepted against my will. They both talked about meeting sometime in the week. They . . . they talked about me as if I was dumb. He told her I was under the mental service because of the bad things I did in the past; that I was a cruel killer full of shit.'

I wanted walking out. The management used Tito's accusation to judge me. Phiona handed me an incident report written by Mohammed. The writing, bold but not legible, narrated what occurred after I left the support home last night.

My eyes tried to read the lines a second time but I couldn't and they wouldn't leave the sheet either. I felt Phiona's eyes on me.

'I do not understand what is going on,' I finally said, letting the paper fall on the desk.

'Tito said you both had coffee with *this* woman,' Phiona said.

'We met with a woman but . . .'

'But your report says nothing of that,' Victor interrupted.

'It wasn't important,' I said.

'We are disappointed in you,' Phiona said, a smile fading on her face.

I walked out of the office dejected, filled with questions. I couldn't explain anything. How do I find another job? I thought of a possible return to Australia.

For two days, I only glanced at Rayleigh's number on my phone, thinking of what to do. My knuckles longed to break Tito's cheekbones. Then I dialled Rayleigh's number on the third day. She agreed to meet with me at the same coffee place in the mall.

I was there 30 minutes before our meet time. She came in five minutes late in a red dress and took the seat opposite me. We had cappuccino. I waited for her to ask of Tito.

She did.

I had never met any white person who pronounced Tito's name as well as Rayleigh did. I hesitated. 'What is your relationship with him?'

'I have no relationship with Tito. I met him for the first time the other day.'

'Liar!' I yelled and got up to my feet. People around stared at me. She stared at me, unmoved. I sat down. 'I am sorry. I lost my job because of that meeting.'

'I am not surprised he knew me. I understand, Michael. I understand how you feel.' Her hand touched mine over the table.

She continued, 'I am certain that there is nothing wrong with the murderer. Tito, his parents in Nigeria, the lawyers they hired, and the entire mental health system in this country are just a stage.'

'What do you mean?'

'I have spent the last couple months searching for the man who killed my sister, Kay. She was murdered in Nigeria. Tito killed Kay and her partner.'

'I am sorry Rayleigh. I don't know what to say. I can be penalised for giving out this statement; Tito hears voices. He claims to hear the voices of his murdered victims and his former pastor. His IQ is too low and places him under some Intellectual Disability Act, which means he cannot go to jail. He is not guilty, on the basis of his mental illness and intellectual disability.'

Her eyes were still for a moment, looking over my shoulders. She nodded, sighed and looked over the table. 'I can't be fooled by this world anymore. The bastard has no mental illness. He is smarter than the judge who placed him under intellectual disability. Tito deserved a death sentence, but he was secretly taken out of Nigeria with the help of the government his parent works for. I guess you know his father is a senator in Nigeria?'

'Yeah. I also know his mother is a minister.'

11.

People poured into the courthouse built twelve years after Nigeria's independence. Only a few of them were relations to any of the accused persons. They mostly came to get ingredients for gossip. The policemen pushed an oyinbo man into the courtroom. The oyinbo struggled to maintain his balance with his cuffed hands and held onto the barrier in front of him. One of the policemen behind him raised a woman's shoe against his face, and when he bent in fright, he was laughed at. This was Gregory Pink. He lived in Nigeria for more than a decade and claimed he knew no other home. He stank of urine smell that came with him from the cell he had been in for the last three days.

People spat, cursed and laughed. Michael imagined himself in Mr Pink's shoes and knew he couldn't carry such weight in his heart and pushed the thought away. A large woman with bulgy eyes, wearing a *gele* on her head, threw a question at the Englishman. She wanted to know if he fancied children too.

Some men in suits entered the courtroom and sat in the front seats before the judge.

'Court!' a man in a blue uniform announced. The judge entered, tailed by a group of policemen. Silence fell over the room. He took his seat, and adjusted his glasses.

They made the Englishman stand.

His lawyer, a huge man in the front row, stood, and said, 'When will we Nigerians grow up? Mr Pink has no enemies here. He has lived in Lagos for the past fifteen years. He brought his business to Nigeria. He brought his good character. Mr Pink is not corrupt. There is, in fact, no evidence that he had sex with a man. It is ludicrous that he is shamed, arrested and brought to court for a crime cooked out of rumours.'

'Objection, my lord, this is nonsense,' a small, skinny man in an ash suit from the front row interrupted, standing to speak. 'Nigeria's history, culture, and values, and most recently, constitution and policies, condemn despicable acts such as homosexuality, which Mr Pink has practised for more than twenty years now. Mr Pink here has been grooming young boys, some as young as sixteen, whose parents can be brought to this court to testify.'

People cheered.

The judged waved his hands. The small, skinny man nodded his head sideways and sat down.

'I plead with you, my lord, to act in the most appropriate way. Mr Pink does not deserve such humiliation. He has not raped a woman, abused a child or committed sodomy. He only admitted to one of the witnesses who I believe would testify against him today, that he had feelings for a male person whom they both knew. The male person in question was never approached by Mr Pink,' Mr Pink's lawyer pleaded.

'Rubbish!' A slim boy, about fourteen or fifteen, who wore a worn singlet and sat in front Michael Merije, screamed.

Michael asked the boy to shut up. 'Who the hell are you?'

The boy stood, attracting stares. He switched to Yoruba and spoke making threatening gestures; he waved his hand over his head, touched his tongue and pointed to the roof, in a manner of swearing to God.

Two policemen approached him. Michael changed seats, moving to the row behind. The clock ran fast. A group of grinning young women walked out of the courtroom.

Mr Pink was led to the stand. He appeared relaxed and ready for any bullet.

'Mr Pink, are you a homosexual?' the skinny lawyer asked.

'No.'

'I don't believe that but we will proceed. Have you lured any other Nigerian man other than Nicholas Epko into this game of yours?' the skinny lawyer asked.

'Objection my lord! This question . . .'

The judge waved off the huge lawyer. 'Mr Pink should answer the question.'

Mr Pink shook his head. 'No.'

Every question that came out of the mouth of the skinny lawyer formed a fist in the air. To Michael, the attacks were punches. He visualised blood spilling out of Mr Pink's mouth.

Mr Nicholas Ekpo was pushed into the courtroom by three policemen. He wore a tight vest. His eyes were bulgy and his brows were broad. He was heavily built, very tall and slightly bent. His reluctance revealed strength. He kicked against the air and used his palms to shield his ears against the voices that filled the courtroom.

'Bring him to the stand,' the skinny lawyer said, in his scathing, husky voice.

A policeman pushed Nicholas forward.

Nicholas charged at him. '*You wan fight*?'

The same policeman jabbed the edge of his rifle on Nicholas' chest. 'Behave!'

Nicholas lost his footing but regained himself immediately.

'Mr Ekpo, did you have a girlfriend or a wife before you met Mr Pink?' the skinny lawyer asked.

Nicholas looked around the courtroom. His eyes met Mr Pink. 'No,' he said.

'Who then is Magdalene Ogeh?'

Nicholas shook his head. 'She belongs to my past.'

'Are you in a homosexual relationship with Mr Pink?'

'No.'

'What relationship do you have with him?'

'I want him to sponsor me abroad,' Nicholas said.

'You just want to go abroad? That's why you let this shameless white monster infect you with his penis?'

'Objection!' The huge lawyer stood up.

Michael couldn't watch the judge wave his hand anymore; the courtroom smelled of sweat; so he walked out and squatted at the entrance gate. Bile rose in his throat and he spat on the ground.

12.

Senator Ogheneovo didn't want his driver or his security escort to see the ugliness of his private life so he discharged them for the day and drove the car himself. He headed for the bar where young university girls hunted for big men. He thought of his wife and blamed her for Tito's tragedies. Anger rose from a valley within him; how he had plans for Tito. He found out Tito's condition earlier and wanted foster parents for him in New Zealand where he would get the right diagnosis and support. Mrs Ogheneovo, a firm believer in miracles, waited for a miracle. Absentminded in his thoughts he drove through a red traffic light. He cursed himself, 'Shit head.' He wasn't elected as a senator to die foolishly.

He felt good being behind the wheels. He swerved the car at sharp turns and overtook other cars in the busy Abuja traffic. His wife loved his rough driving when they were younger. The first time he drove her in a car, from Benin to Warri, he recalled telling her she would become a big woman one day. He forced a principal into retirement so that she could become the first female principal of that government girl's college in Warri. He pointed a pistol at an electoral officer and asked him to burn ballot papers in an election to secure Mrs Ogheneovo's seat in the House of Representatives. The same woman now challenged him openly; one time, in front of the President. Her skin didn't taste like candy anymore. He could go live on AIT and renounce his love for her. He once loved to cuddle her in the back seat of his 504 Peugeot in the middle of nowhere or in the outskirts of Benin. Now a minister, she could buy her way anywhere with the tricks he taught her. She had secret bank accounts in New Zealand, Australia and China, and kept them away from him. It was a hungry and unscrupulous journalist, as they came, who threatened to expose her with these secrets. But he sealed his lips with money. Senator Ogheneovo never raised the issue with his wife. She surprised him when she got Tito out of Nigeria to New Zealand. Tito, eligible for an invalid's benefit and a quiet life in New Zealand, seemed more like a freed prisoner. He was dumbfounded how she convinced the Nigerian judiciary to hand Tito over to the government of New Zealand.

He stopped at a roundabout. An Abuja commercial bus, painted green with white stripes, pulled up beside him. He thought of his first marriage. The blue-eyed Jessica Crossly. He thought about her four boys he fathered for almost two years; how he picked them up from school to win her heart while she was a busy as a saleswoman at the mall in Central Christchurch. He wound down the window, spat out a glob of saliva; some spittle hung in his beard and smeared the side of the car's door. He cleaned his beard with the back of his hand. He didn't see the truck when he proceeded. He ran into it. His body flung onto the cracked windscreen.

He didn't die. He sank into unconsciousness. He dreamt of his life as a younger man in New Zealand still married to Jessica. She arrived from work and asked after the children. He forgot to pick them up from school. He hated her voice whenever she got upset.

He opened his eyes and found himself in a room of white walls and red curtains. Two men chatted and laughed at the top of their voices. His nose picked up the smell of antiseptic. He felt immense pressure on his left thigh and tried to move it but he couldn't. He groaned. The men's laughter quietened. They were his friends. The Minister of Finance and Chief Efe Walter. He smiled at them. These men were behind most rumours about the President.

'They couldn't kill the lion. He is back awake, and ready to roar,' Chief Walter said, laughing. 'How are you, great one?'

'Ahh. Honourable Senator, welcome back from hell,' the minister added.

'The laughter of scallywags got me out of swoon.'

'We celebrate you, Senator. The evil powers of your village couldn't get you,' the Chief said. 'You are okay. No shit to worry about.'

He could feel the tautness around his head and the sting over his right shoulder. 'Did I only pass out?'

'Senator, which witch-doctor do you pay . . .' the minister shook his head and laughed, '. . that couldn't protect you against accidents? I should take you to my village where all charms have roots. For protection.'

The senator chuckled.

'Your wife will be here anytime soon . . . but we would like to know what you were doing without security. What happened to that your short driver? Maybe you wanted your body to be eaten by vultures,' the minister said.

On the mention of his wife, he felt his heart go numb.

She arrived while he was on the phone. The glow of her ebony skin now lay in a bin in his heart. She gestured at the policemen who arrived with her and they went back outside the room.

The Finance Minister and Chief Walter got to their feet.

'Indeed the lioness is here. The only woman from Warri in the cabinet.'

'Chief Walter, don't start again,' she replied, her attention on her husband on the bed.

'He is alright, Madam. Just ensure he eats enough starch and *banga* with a whole goat after he is discharged. I bet he was on his way to a pepper soup joint when he hit the truck,' the Finance Minister said.

The men left while the senator was still on the phone. Their laughter faded and sirens wailed outside for a while.

She waited. It was obvious he was on the phone with the president. She stared at his bandaged head and then his thigh. She wondered if she cared. He laughed and pressed the phone harder against his ear. Laughing and yet, just hours ago, he could have been in hell. All politicians go to hell if they don't repent, a preacher once told her. She sowed more money into the said preacher's life and he prayed that she would make eternity.

'I appreciate this call, your Excellency. I do not think this demands a check-up overseas. I will only have a couple of days off,' he said. He replaced the phone by the side and relaxed his head on the softness of the pillow.

'How are you?' she asked.

He closed his eyes and replied, 'I think I am okay.'

'What went into your head? When was the last time you drove?'

He sighed. 'I can drive any car in any part of this world.'

'You are lucky God was on your side.'

A middle-aged man walked in. His whiskers were tousled. His tie hung casually. 'I am Dr Mahmud, madam,' he said, not looking at her but at her husband. 'And sir, I have been the one looking after you.'

'Oh. Thank you for not making this woman a widow,' the senator said, laughing.

Dr Mahmud raised an eyebrow and smiled. 'Madam, your husband is a free man now. I cannot hold him here any longer. Just few bruises and cuts. Senator, you lost a lot of blood, but you have a good heart. Transfusion wasn't needed. You will have to visit us often so we can keep checking for any sign of concussion. If you experience any distortion of your memory or unusual dizziness, please, give me a call.'

* * *

He wanted to say *'No! Not again...'*

'Where were you going?' she repeated her question. He knew she suspected that he kept a woman somewhere. The absence of his driver and security was enough for her to conclude.

He looked through his side window. Three women argued outside.

'God's mercy on your soul.'

'Did you come to pick me up so we could start a quarrel? For chrissake, woman! Where is your empathy, what happened to the woman I married twenty-five years ago?'

'I should ask you the same question.'

'Okay. Ask then. And I will give you a reply.'

She sighed.

He listened to the siren for a while. He hated himself instantly for getting into the car with her. It was her convoy. But somehow, they still needed each other, if not for anything, their children whom they always wanted to groom for politics.

* * *

In the days before Tito murdered the lesbian lovers, a treacherous premonition haunted his mother. One night she believed her husband had snuck out of the house to be with a mistress. Her wrapper came loose as she tried to sleep. An owl hooted. She adjusted her body. It felt as if someone loosened the knot of her wrapper. She wondered if her husband had returned, maybe his mistress didn't hold him back for long that time around. The smell of alcohol was absent; the smell of his body was different, but familiar. She felt fingers tickle her between her thighs and she gasped, stretched and opened her eyes. Tito. She screamed and sprang up, breathing hard.

The night was quiet. Her husband was asleep beside her and Tito was absent. She kept this dream a secret. She once dreamt of her mother dressed in a colourful *aso oke*, waving goodbye to her. A fortnight later, news came from the village that her mother in-law died of snakebite. She avoided Tito for the next few days: she came home late when he was in bed and left for work early before he woke. One Saturday morning, he came into the bedroom. She barely had a towel around her body. She stopped drying her hair. He mumbled something.

'What are you saying?' she asked.

'Mummy . . . I am tired of life. I hate myself. Daddy does not want me to play football. He won't let any of the drivers take me to the pitch.'

She watched his lips. She watched his eyes. They were searching her body. She prayed in her heart.

'What do you want, Tito?'

He turned around and left her room.

Tears filled her eyes.

Six months later Tito was living in New Zealand. Mrs Ogheneovo was in the country for a second visit and she is with Nina this time. Her son's troubles were forgotten and New Zealand covered her shame and kept Tito quiet, even though the country never appealled to her, never appeared beautiful, as everyone said.

She drove the hired car on the Albany Highway. Her eyes were wet with memories; Nina's imagination, filled with questions.

The car slowly reached a roundabout and she took the second exit unsure about the location, though she kept driving. The GPS prompted them that they were at their destination. She parked her vehicle. There were two buildings in the remote location, unlike the last time. 'There used to be just one building,' she muttered.

The buildings were identical, a wooden fence built around both. She and Nina went through the gate and she re-familiarised herself with the sound of the lake behind the building. Two men led them in.

They sat on a couch with Tito. Mrs Ogheneovo's eyes were filled with tears. Nina quivered beside her.

'I guess you have adjusted to life here, Tito?' she asked.

Tito didn't reply.

She asked Nina to sing him a song. Nina started incoherently but got on well.

'Continue, dear daughter.'

When we leave this world
When we leave this world . . .

We only smile
Knowing there's somewhere . . .

'Please stop!' Tito shouted

Nina stopped singing.

'Go away,' he said.

One of the staff members approached the visitors and said, 'He has asked both of you to leave.'

Tito placed his palms over his face.

'I have my visiting hours here until five pm. We came all the way from Nigeria to visit my son,' his mother said.

'But he has insisted that you two leave,' the man said.

'Do you know my son more than I do?'

The man walked away, indifferent.

Then Tito reached for Nina, who jumped to her feet at the surprise. She wasn't quick enough to move away. Tito caught her hair, yanked it backwards and slammed her forehead on the wall.

His mother rose to her feet and looked around for help. The man she failed to listen to wasn't nearby.

Tito soon faced his mother and she saw the venom in his eyes. His fingers clawed her face. Two men emerged and took hold of Tito's arms. He swore and kicked the air.

'Go out! The two of you! Go and stay in the car outside, please,' one of the men said.

* * *

Mr Ogheneovo was sure his wife and daughter were still with Tito. When he saw the light of his cell phone come on by his side, he wondered if Tito was finally lured to speak to him.

He gestured at the driver to turn off the stereo before he answered the call.

He heard Nina crying and fear gripped him.

'Daddy, Daddy, Tito attacked us! He . . .'

'Hey Nina, calm down. Where is your mother?'

'She is here. We are inside the car, outside the support home.'

'Let me speak to her, please.'

'Okay, hold on.'

He cradled his head in his palm, hating the day.

'She won't speak now, Daddy. She's crying.'

'Tell me what happened. Calm down and tell me what happened, Nina.'

'Mummy asked me to sing for him, and . . . and . . .'

'Calm down, Nina. I am on my way to the office right now. I will call back.'

In the office, he asked his secretary to cancel the morning meetings. He pulled open his drawer and stared at his New Zealand passport. He wished Jessica stayed away from cigarettes when he brought her to Nigeria to meet his parents in '79.

13.

Tito's movement on the stairs was slow but loud. Ejiro and Kay ran into the kitchen and locked themselves in. They clung to each other as the intruder's fists came hard against the door. Helpless, they crept underneath the kitchen sink.

Both women had recently paid an orphan's university tuition. What then did that sudden attack portend? They hadn't hurt or abused anyone. They shut their ears against Tito's threats.

'My dream is to see her become independent in life,' Kay replied, when the police asked her about the orphan. 'I didn't leave England for Nigeria to turn girls to lesbians.'

'We are just doing our part to maintain law and order. It is good that we have heard your say on this. We will convey your message to the worried relatives of the girl,' one of the policewomen said.

Tito hit the door again and both women jolted.

A third hit brought the door down. A shelf yards from the stove crashed to the ground. The women's screams died as Tito neared them.

Kay's eyes, widened with fear, stared at his boots. Ejiro shivered and kept her eyes closed.

Tito reached for Kay and pulled her out. He pushed her against the fallen shelf and stabbed her on her arm with a knife. She screamed. Blood splattered on his face. The knife tore through her arm and into the wooden board. He left her lying almost lifeless on the floor. He stepped in front of the sink where Ejiro curled herself under, her eyes shut as she trembled.

He strained his ears to pick what she was saying.

'Now you remember the Virgin Mary?' he said.

'Please, let her live and take me instead,' Kay said in a weak voice from where her arm remained pinned.

'I came for both of you,' Tito replied, not glancing at Kay. He dragged Ejiro out. 'Filth,' he muttered.

'Please . . . Please,' Ejiro whispered.

'You bitches are full of filth, full of shit,' he shouted and tossed Ejiro over the sink.

The faucet almost drove into her head. The sink broke off the wall and shattered on the tiled floor. Ejiro lied motionless on the floor, her torn scalp sticky with blood. Water ran over the floor flushing with blood everywhere. Tito's shadow went back over Kay. In the darkness, the clock ticked and death met the women.

14.

Tito took a seat at the dining and fought the urge to take a banana out of the fruit bowl before him. He looked at the clock on the far wall beside a framed watercolour painting and wished he could read the clock like the digital wristwatch he kept in his room. The long hand on the clock pointed at two, and the short hand pointed between four and five.

Someone pushed the door open. Ruru, who maintained the garden at Mount Eden, entered. Many patients could not keep the job like Ruru. They were always dismissed for stalking or assaulting a co-worker. Ruru stood on the doorway for a while to search his pockets.

'It seems you are late,' Tito said.

Ruru glanced at him and said, 'Michael didn't come to pick me up on time.' He got his key out of his breast pocket and headed for his room at the far end.

Shortly afterwards, Michael came in through the door Ruru left ajar.

'What have you been doing with yourself, Tito?' Michael asked and looked around. He walked into the lobby and sat on a sofa.

Tito did not reply.

'We have always told you to behave well, treat people fine, mind your bizzo and you will get more functions to attend, but nope, you think you know everything.'

'I am okay, and will never set foot on that damn Woodland ground,' Tito said.

'You got kicked out of Woodland for hitting Austin and causing him to lose an eye.' Michael sat up and reached for the television remote on the side table. 'Now you say – *I am okay, and will never set foot on that damn Woodland ground*.'

Ruru came into the lobby holding a duffel bag with cables hanging out. 'I want to play my game,' he said.

'Have you done your chores, mate?' Michael asked. 'You must tidy your room and clean the bathroom before I grant your request. Ruru let the duffel bag fall to the floor. He caught Tito's stare on him as he walked back to his room.

Before the passage that led to the courtyard was a notice that Phiona instructed Michael to place on the wall. TITO MUST NOT BE ALLOWED TO PLAY SOCCER VIDEO GAMES. NO STAFF OR PATIENT SHOULD DISCUSS SOCCER IN THE HOUSE WITH TITO.

Ruru applied the bleach over the toilet seat and wiped it with a folded tissue. He mopped the floor from one end to the other and went back to the lobby.

Michael seemed captured by the six pm news. Ruru, scared to be told *no* a second time, did not reiterate his request. Instead, he went out into the courtyard where his *pohutukawa* tree grew healthily. He sat on a bench and watched the breeze stir the green leaves. He had asked the management to get him this plant after seeing a documentary on the plant on Maori TV. His pohutukawa tree would defend him against Tito one of these days.

'Ruru,' Michael called from inside. 'Come play your game if you have completed your chores.'

Ruru went back into the lobby and Tito wasn't there anymore.

Ruru connected the game to the television.

Michael sat by and watched Ruru play his Play Station car racing game. He had lost this job and begun to apply for other jobs. No employer called him for an interview. He thought of going back to Sydney. If Tito's care manager didn't show up in the parking lot in front of the Railway campus where he lived, he would have boarded the night flight back to Australia. The visit baffled him but he couldn't turn down the request. Victor gestured at him to get into the passenger seat of the Mitsubishi L200 and offered him a higher salary just to return to work and help in supporting Tito. Michael never expected this. Back on the job, with Tito in a newly built facility, Michael realised that he lacked motivation. He slept on duty and didn't care.

Ruru paused the video game, distanced himself a few metres and farted.

Michael shut his eyes and pretended not to hear the fart. He fell asleep and woke up an hour later to see a blank television screen. His watch read nine o'clock. He got up, glanced at the passage that led to the rooms of Tito and Ruru, and then he turned off the lights.

* * *

Ruru was about to enter his room when he heard Tito's door open behind him. His heart skipped a beat. He stood, listening to Tito's feet from behind.

'Go in, man, and stop standing there like a police officer,' Tito whispered.

He went in and Tito followed him. 'Michael is still in the lobby,' Ruru said.

'I know. He is getting paid by the management for sleeping at work.'

Ruru let his duffel bag containing his video game fall on the rug and walked toward the window, drawing the separated curtains to shield the light falling through.

'I hate this country,' Tito said.

'Go back to Africa.'

'My parents think my life is in danger over there.' Tito sighed and sat on the bed, rubbing his fingers over Ruru's sheet.

'You could get deported from New Zealand, you know?' said Ruru.

'I am a citizen. My dad came to New Zealand long ago and married a Kiwi woman. He became a citizen but later divorced her and went back to Nigeria where he married my mother. I have dual nationalities.'

'I got German blood in me because my father's mother was German. Do you think I could go there and live when I am released?'

'Maybe.' Tito got up and walked toward Ruru. 'You know why I am here, Ruru? Don't waste time, please.'

'This can't continue, bro.'

'I can't help it.'

Ruru turned around and caught Tito's gaze.

'Come on, Ruru,' Tito said and pointed at his groin.

'No. Tito, No.'

Tito widened his eyes and rested his hands on his waist. 'Don't let me down or I will kill you,' Tito whispered. 'You know why I ended up here in New Zealand?'

Ruru looked at the ceiling. He nodded his head and grudgingly knelt in front of Tito. His fingers trembled as they found Tito's zip.

'Come on, Ruru,' Tito said, looking up. He closed his eyes and swallowed as Ruru's spittle collided with his phallus. Ruru hesitated. Tito opened his eyes, looked downwards and struck Ruru's face with a fist.

Ruru fell to the floor and groaned quietly. Tito zipped himself up. He kicked Ruru in the ribs.

'Argghhh! Please . . .'

'You are full of shit, faggot!' Tito said and spat on Ruru. Put your head right in front of me!'

Ruru adjusted himself. He squatted this time.

Tito stood firmer this time, his legs spread apart. He undid his zip and felt his limpness. He pissed over Ruru's face and sighed as the last drops of cum splattered over the rug. He pushed Ruru away and walked out of the room leaving the door ajar.

The next morning, Ruru woke up early. He stank of piss. The room stank. He sniffed, pushed his fingers against the rug and stood to his feet. The door was still ajar. He walked toward his wardrobe and took out a clean pair of jeans and his green baseball jersey before heading for the bathroom.

He used cold water from the shower at first, massaging parts of his body that hurt from last night. He poured some shower milk over his sponge, scrubbed his skin and rinsed himself with hot water. He towelled his body and got dressed. He brushed his hair and headed to the courtyard where he saw Michael smoking.

'What happened to your tree, Ruru?' Michael asked.

The large pot that held his pohutukawa tree was broken into bits and its black soil stared at him like shit. The leaves were scattered over the courtyard and its branches and stems broken into bits. Ruru picked a broken branch and cried.

'I will go and talk to Tito right now,' Michael said, rubbing the end of his cigarette on the bench to kill the fire. He walked into the house, inserted a key into Tito's door and pushed it open.

'What the hell!' Tito said, alarmed, sitting up with his hands behind him.

'What did you do to Ruru's tree?'

'Nothing. I did nothing.'

'You better say the truth because Phiona will get involved.'

'That's good. She is going to know how you sleep all the time without doing your job.'

Michael nodded and slammed the door. He turned around and rested his back on the door. He needed more tobacco. Tito and the job had turned him into a smoker overnight.

He walked back to the courtyard and did not find Ruru. He went back inside the building and called Ruru twice. Outside, the gate wobbled awkwardly; the hinges on one end ripped from the fence. Michael took out his cell phone and dialled.

* * *

Phiona's entered the driveway with the clinical manager in her red Chevrolet. She parked the car yards away and they walked toward the gate.

Phiona's gaze was on the hinges of the gate that hung disjointedly from the fence. Diana faced Michael, whose hands searched for warmth in his pockets.

'Where is Tito?' Diane asked.

'He has been shattering the windows and bringing down all the pantries and cupboards inside. I had to lock him up in there.'

'Really,' Diane said, and turned around to face Phiona.

'When did he start that, Michael?' Phiona asked.

'Just after I alerted you about Ruru.'

A shattering sound rang in the house. A television broke out through the lounge window and landed twelve yards in front of them. Diana shuddered. Michael stared at the shattered television.

Phiona's phone rang and she stepped away to answer the call. 'Phiona here.' The police wanted some details about Ruru.

'He is half Maori, with dark curly hair, diagnosed with Asperger's syndrome. He appeared in court four years ago for attempting to rape a neighbour. My manager, from recent assessments, believes that there is seventy per cent probability that he might reoffend and—' Another shattering sound within the building caused her to pause. 'Please, can you send some of your men over? The other patient in the facility is causing us hell.' She turned around and spotted Michael going toward the building.

* * *

Ruru sat on a bench in the train station and looked around. He caught the gaze of a Chinese girl and felt indecisive about waiting for a train with no cash in his pockets. The Chinese girl walked to the ladies' room and he followed her. He walked past a group of loud women. He pushed open the door of the ladies' room and sighted the rear view of the Chinese woman walking into one of the smaller cubicles. She turned around, smiled and approached him. 'The men's room is on the other side,' she said pointing over his shoulder.

Ruru didn't move; instead, he closed the door behind him and walked toward her. Before she could yell, his palm covered her mouth. He pushed her into the cubicle and forced his hand under her skirt. She sucked her lower lip and remained quiet. He let his pants fall, raised her leg up, and thrust himself against her quavering body.

* * *

Phiona hated to deal with the police. She sat at the Henderson police station on a desk facing Tito. He wouldn't talk. Michael stood beside one of the policemen, who had intervened in Tito's escalating behaviour.

Tony, the police officer Phiona had dated years ago, came in.

'We have the second kid now.'

Relief washed over her. She stood up. Tony led her out of the room into a corridor.

'He raped a woman before we found him.'

'Oh, hell no!' she lamented and followed him. 'This has completely made a fool out of me, Tony!' She thought of quitting her role, which had taken her twelve years to attain.

Tony walked ahead of her as if the news meant nothing. She followed him into a room.

A policewoman, in her mid-thirties, was talking to Ruru.

The woman turned around, and said, 'Hello Phiona, I'm Jenny.' She looked at Tony and said, 'There is something else.'

Tony raised a brow.

Jenny, a smallish woman with short blond hair, said to Ruru, 'Tell them what you just told me.'

Ruru nodded his head. Tears filled his eyes. He finally spoke about Tito. 'He threatened to kill me . . . He has been doing it, but I have been too scared. Too scared to say anything.'

'I need a seat, Tony,' Phiona said. 'Please.'

15.

The flames climbed up the walls toward the ceiling and filled the bathroom. She peered in the blurriness. The flame in the form of a devil's wings breathed on her. She let some cold water rush against her thighs, slouched in the bathtub. Ejiro got out of the bathtub and opened the shelf over the basin on which Kay's gel, scissors, lipsticks, creams, nail files and combs lay. She grabbed a scissors and slouched back in the half-filled bathtub of water. She rubbed one of the scissors' blades against her left wrist in search of a vein. She dipped the wrist into the warm water and slit it, and then placed the scissors on the edge of the bath. She wanted to laugh at her clumsiness, but she let out a moan.

She heard Kay's movements in their bedroom and the bathroom door opened.

'Gosh, what are you doing to yourself?' Kay lamented.

Kay reached for Ejiro. She took Ejiro's bleeding wrist and shoved the scissors from the edge of the bathtub to the floor.

'Don't be so stupid. Don't be so stupid. I cannot believe this. What do you want to do to yourself?' Kay went on.

'Why do I have to live?' Ejiro asked.

'You are being so stupid and annoying.' Kay helped her out of the bathtub. Water dripped from both their bodies to the floor. 'Forget about yesterday? Come on, Ejiro!' Kay led Ejiro to the bedroom and made her sit in front of their mirror. She brought the stool with a brown leather cushion close to Ejiro, sat and reached for a drawer where she brought out a box. She took a chunk of cotton wool from the box, placed it over the torn skin and pressed hard. She opened the bottle of methylated spirit, and its strong smell filled the room. She dripped it over the cotton wool, over the cut, and watched Ejiro twitch at its effect.

'Why do you do this, Kay? You made me think I made a mistake. You made me think I had become so ugly that you now hated me.'

'How can I, Ejiro?'

'Why hide it from me?'

Kay shook her head. 'What is the point of telling you something that isn't worth talking about? It would only hurt you.'

'Tell me, Kay. Have you started seeing someone?'

Kay pressed the cotton wool on the cut.

'Tell me, Kay. Who is he?'

Kay left the cotton wool for Ejiro to manage, then she stood up. 'I am seeing nobody.' She looked at their images in the mirror and placed her hands on Ejiro's shoulders. The wetness over Ejiro's limbs and breasts dried. Her breasts were not as supple as they used to be in their small roundish shape. And Kay remembered how Ejiro's beautiful dark pupils always flashed with joyful proclamations. 'Remember when we first met and we had a brawl about your religious views, Ejiro?'

Ejiro nodded.

'Remember days you convinced me to go to church with you?' Kay left Ejiro's shoulders and sighed. 'I thought you were suffering then. I pitied you. Now, living in your world where everyone lives by the Bible or Koran, you have backslidden completely. For me, I now desire to discover my spirituality.'

'Did you get involved with a man in that church?'

Kay shook her head, frustrated over Ejiro's gaze.

'No, Ejiro,' Kay said, her eyes turned away from the mirror. 'I went there because I wanted to look at things the way you did before we met.'

'And who did you meet in church? You must have met someone. A man.'

'Stop that, Ejiro.'

'I am not a kid, Kay.'

'The pastor approached me. He said he wanted to talk to me.' Kay applied pressure on Ejiro's cut. 'I met him after a service weeks ago. He told me how pleased he was to have me in his church. And said he would like me to be in church every Sunday. I went there on some Sundays as you know, and met some nice people. I really loved it until I got the note.'

'What note?'

'A note from the pastor.'

'And you never told me?'

'I didn't want you to flare up, Ejiro.'

'What was in it? Where is it?'

'I threw it in the fire where we burn the rubbish.'

Ejiro's eyes widened. She twisted her body on the chair. 'How could you?'

'It's not what you think, Ejiro. I stopped going to the church for our sake. The note spoke of nothing. He wanted to find out why I missed church on some Sundays. I wondered if he knew every member of his congregation and sent them such notes.'

'And you stopped going to the church?'

'Yes.'

'But you met him last night and didn't say?'

'We met at Paddy's.' She hated the sound of Ejiro's voice when it sounded this way. 'I had to, so I could tell him off. His response was like a threat. He threatened me with hell, Ejiro.'

'And you became born-again?'

'Don't mock me, Ejiro. I told him I would face God myself.'

Kay curled on her side of the bed. It wasn't Ejiro's slow snoring that kept her awake; she felt guilty and dirty she couldn't tell Ejiro everything. She got rid of the scissors, the nail files, and even the pins for her ribbon in the bathroom. She took the knives in the kitchen and locked them in a drawer.

She had walked into Paddy's Restaurant the previous night and nearly lost her footing as people stared at her. The pastor sat in one corner in his oversized grey suit and a tie of many colours.

'I am sorry, I . . .'

'It's okay. Men are used to waiting.'

She couldn't stare at him. It felt like staring at her doubts in God.

His fork clanked hard against the plate, making erratic sounds. She endured it.

'You need to establish a relationship with Jesus,' he said, and wiped his mouth with a serviette.

'Who said I don't have one?'

'It's obvious.'

She gave him a distant and scrutinised look. 'How is it obvious?'

'Who is Jesus to you?'

'A man who lived centuries ago.'

His brows rose.

'A prophet, a good man,' she added.

'Is that all?'

'What else do you want to hear, Mr Pastor?'

'Jesus is God, Miss.'

'No, he's not.' The masticated rice in her mouth almost went down the wrong way. She took a serviette and covered her lips. 'I admit I have not been a churchgoer in life but from my little knowledge I hear he is the son of God.'

She met his frozen stare.

'Miss, you have to believe he is God so that your soul does not go to hell when you depart from the world.'

'You seem absolutely sure that I shall go to hell. Maybe you are right. I came to the church to meet good people and listen to some good spiritual views. Can we talk of something else, if you don't mind?'

'I was hoping it would come to this. Separating God from our lifestyle has been the cause of the world's acceptance of fornication, abortion, marijuana and homosexuality.'

She sighed, glancing away from him.

'I am sorry, Miss, but it is inappropriate to be in a same-sex affair. You see, people talk.'

'I am sorry, I need to leave. I don't want to discuss my personal life,' she said.

His held her hands. No man had touched her that way for a long time. She looked around, mindful of the people present.

'Only a man who loves you would tell you this,' he said.

Her eyes fell on his hand still over hers. 'Please,' she said, and withdrew her hands. She fetched her handbag. 'Thanks for the meal.' It was a long walk to the door.

* * *

Ejiro woke from a dream by a noise that pricked her eardrums. Kay remained asleep: the distance between them colossal, unlike the times when she fell asleep with her head on Kay's chest. Ejiro's hand reached for Kay's body.

Kay sat up and her hair fell over her face. 'What's that noise?'

'That's the reason I woke you,' Ejiro whispered, her voice fractured.

Kay got off the bed, her pyjamas top a little rumpled. She turned on the lights and walked toward the window. She pushed the curtains aside and held her breath. Ejiro came up behind her.

'Shit!' Ejiro lamented.

Kay turned around, her palms over her mouth.

The security lights over the gates glowed dimly. At the gate were followers of the pastor Kay recently dined with. They chanted meaningless words and some marched in circles. Two women sang a war-like song loudly. Kay caught the figure of the pastor dressed in a pair of shorts and a sleeveless shirt. He wasn't calm like he was at Paddy's two days ago. He chanted and jumped repeatedly like a mad man. Kay strained her ears to pick out their words. *I bind the spirits of dogs in this house, in the name of Jesus! I break down every trick of Satan and his kingdom*.

'I will go and talk to them,' Kay said. She hurried out of the room and approached gate.

'Please, leave us alone or I will call the police,' she shouted at them.

They ignored her and chanted louder. The pastor didn't look in her direction.

'You are frightening the entire neighbourhood,' Kay said.

One of the men came forward and gripped the gate. His shadow fell over her. 'I command the spirit of repentance to fall over you, in the name of Jesus,' he said.

She stepped backward and ran back to the house to make a call.

Ejiro was wore a green polo shirt and a pair of jeans folded at her knees.

'Police calls are useless in this country,' Ejiro said. 'I am going to chase them away. They are not the only radicals in the world.'

'How are you going to do that?' Kay asked.

'Watch me,' Ejiro replied.

Kay let the phone and followed Ejiro to the unruliness at the gate.

Ejiro headed toward her parked Mercedes and picked up the nozzle of a long hose she used for washing her car in the mornings. She turned on the tap and went toward the praying warriors, who scattered as she bathed them in a splash of water. The chants ceased. She aimed at the pastor and the glasses on his face came off in the darkness. One of the praying men dragged the pastor away.

16.

The rented car came to halt in front of the building. Michael stepped out of it and walked to the entrance, both hands in his jeans pockets. He loved the flowers that lined the sidewalk.

A woman at the reception smiled at him when he came out of the elevator on the second floor.

'Hello, sir. How can I help you?'

'I am Michael Merije and I am here to see one of the weightlifters. Paul Yamo.'

'Oh, hang on, let me check the list,' she said, and opened a file. 'How far have you come, sir?'

'Sydney.'

'You must be exhausted,' she said and traced her finger down the list she found.

'I am. It's a four and a half hour flight.'

'Mr Yamo is expecting you. I will call him now,' she said and picked up the receiver on her desk.

'Ta. I will be out there, waiting,' he said, pointing at the balcony.

'Enjoy your stay in Perth,' she said. The woman watched him walk away while she spoke into the receiver.

Michael stood in front of the aquarium in the balcony. He was attractive, tall and slim, a breakaway from the muscly male occupants in the hotel.

The elevator opened and Paul Yamo, Polynesian weightlifter, stepped from it and approached her. His built muscles restricted a more relaxed movement of his body. She pointed at the visitor in the balcony and Paul walked in the direction. Michael turned around with a big smile and the receptionist saw them kiss each other.

Paul saw her staring. 'It seems someone has her eyes on you,' he whispered to Michael.

'She knows now that I am not straight.'

Paul pulled Michael toward the elevator. 'You need a beer.'

* * *

They walked into a bar where many other muscled men sat at different tables. Each table they passed, Paul announced, 'My man just arrived from Sydney.'

Paul chose a table at the end on the right. He placed orders and pointed to the biggest man in the bar, who had two skinny women at his table. 'That's McGregor. He is yet to contest. Most of us here are climbing up the ladder gradually, struggling between 165 and 170 kg. His coach won't let him contest until the final stages – with the starting weight of 200 kg.'

'Where is he from?'

'Adelaide,' Paul replied. 'It is certain he will be in the Olympics. I am betting on becoming 200 kg, too. So if the sun shines on me I will be in London too. Right now, the target is to do well here and qualify for Melbourne.'

'How have you been doing, though?'

'Not too bad. Not every son of a bitch is a weightlifter, Michael,' Paul said, sipping his drink.

* * *

Michael changed into a pair of black pyjamas and lounged on the bed as he zapped through some television channels.

Paul came in from the bathroom, bare-chested, in a pair of white shorts and sat on the bed.

'Come on, Paul,' Michael said. 'Do the usual thing. It is damn too hot, tonight.'

'This isn't Sydney.'

'Come on, Paul.'

'You know I don't fancy it, but I don't want you nagging so I will go and put them on.' He got up and put on his pyjamas top and pants. They were the same design and colour as Michael's. He went back to bed.

'Don't we look like lovers now?' Michael asked.

'We look like twins, Michael,' Paul replied and narrowed his eyes to catch the subtitle of an interview with Kim Jong-un on TV.

Michael didn't like the reply. He took his phone from underneath his pillow and scrolled through his notifications.

Paul took off the sheets and got off the bed. Michael snored in his curled position. Paul quietly changed from pyjamas into his training gear. Track pants. Black singlet. Brown sneakers. He stepped out to the ground floor where the gym was. He spent the next three hours training intensely. Before dawn, two of his mates walked into the gym – red-haired Sam and tall Goowie.

'Thought you might be on that chocolate boy of yours,' Sam said.

The 60 kg in Paul's hands felt like 200 kg.

Goowie laughed. Both men went into separate bathrooms in the right section of the gym. The sound of the showers infuriated Paul. He struggled to his feet, didn't shower as intended, and left for his room. Michael was still in bed.

Michael sat up when Paul came out of the bathroom minutes later with a white towel hanging over his neck.

'Where did you go?'

'You are up. The gym.'

'I can't wait to watch you win, Paul.'

Paul thought of Sam's words in the gym, caught Michael's stare and looked away. He opened the wardrobe and searched for a jumper.

* * *

Michael applauded like everyone else but not really in excitement over McGregor's first appearance. McGregor climbed the stage calmly, fetched a bit of powder and confronted the weight. He massaged the rod that held two discs of a hundred kilograms on each side. He lifted it with little effort, up to his chest, and with a quick grunt, he raised it over his head and showed his strength. The applause of the spectators rose in thunderously.

Michael expected Paul to be the second man for the day. It turned out to be a red-haired Caucasian with a long beard who confronted the

160 kg after powdering his hands and lifted it over his chest. He staggered a little, lifted the weight over his head but didn't get it right. Three red lights flickered.

As he left backstage, the red-haired weightlifter brushed his shoulder against Paul who was on his way onto the stage. 'Bloody poofter,' he said.

Paul turned around and looked at him. It was Sam again. Paul wanted to grip his throat and push him to the floor; and if possible bring down a dumbbell over the idiot's head.

Paul felt a hand on his back and he turned around.

'They are waiting,' his coach said.

He climbed the stage and rubbed powder in his palms. '175 kg,' he muttered and hit his chest repeatedly. He wanted to make Michael proud and get back at Sam. He lifted the weight to his chest, groaned and felt the strain in his clavicles.

A few spectators cheered. Michael stood up from where he sat and cheered.

Air filled Paul's mouth and his eyes bulged. He lifted the monstrosity of metal over his head and grunted. But it overpowered the strength in his arms and thundered down as he fell.

The judges' lights went red.

Paul struggled to his feet, saw Michael's disappointment and left the stage.

* * *

Paul folded his arms. His eyes distant as he rested his weight on the car parked in front of the hotel.

'You should have tried the second time. You shouldn't have given up,' Michael said.

'Why did you come here?' Paul asked. 'Did you come here to take over my manager's job?'

'Paul, your loss is my loss.'

'No Michael,' Paul said. 'My loss is my bloody loss! Stay away from my career.' His voice was firm at first but it broke. He turned his back to Michael.

'Has it come to this, Paul? Has it come to this? He drew near Paul and touched him. 'Turn around and look at me.'

'Don't touch me!' Paul said. 'Don't touch me, Michael. You are the reason I failed today.'

Michael bit his lower lip and nodded. A weightlifter came out of the hotel, entered a white Chevrolet and drove away. 'I will leave for the airport now. You are still in the best losers category and I wouldn't like to ruin that for you.'

Michael walked to the car and entered it. 'Get out of the way.'

Paul gave way and wiped his face. 'Aren't you taking your luggage?'

'Bring it back with you,' Michael replied and turned on the car's ignition.

17.

Kay picked up the phone. She listened for a while and covered her mouth in shock. She spoke briefly and hung up. She caught Ejiro's stare. Ejiro was slouched on the sofa, her legs crossed on the table.

Ejiro took the remote on her lap and muted the television.

'Mama Afoke is dead,' Kay said.

'Are you serious?'

'It was your uncle Greg on the phone. He didn't have much time. Said the funeral is tomorrow. He has offered his home to us for the night - if we decide to attend.'

'I don't feel any sympathy for the witch.'

'Ejiro!'

'What?'

'She just died.'

Ejiro laughed. She walked to the dining, opened the slender fridge and brought out a can of beer. 'I hate this feeling building up in me. I should be screaming in joy.'

'Stop that, Ejiro. Stop it. Stop it.'

Ejiro filled her glass. 'Do you want a drink?'

'No, thank you.'

'Why should I feel hurt? We picked her up from the roadside in the village, brought her to Warri, gave her a life and at the end, she went back to the village and told everybody how lesbians make love!'

'At least she helped put the house in order.'

'She did shit! I always re-tidied the entire house each time she claimed to have done a wonderful job. I am not going, Kay.'

'Are you out of your mind?'

The next morning, Ejiro wore a fitted black dress that barely reached her knees, took their small luggage, which she put in the trunk of the Mercedes, and waited for Kay.

'Sorry, sweetie,' Kay said as she finally entered the car.

'We still have time. I have this nagging headache,' Ejiro said.

'It's the beer you took last night. I will drive if you . . .'

'No. I can still drive.'

Ejiro inserted a disc in the stereo.

'Please, can you play something else?' Kay requested.

'I want this one.'

'Ejiro, please, play anything else. Not rap.'

'You aren't stopping me.'

The silence between them, punctuated by Nigerian rap songs, lingered as the car sailed into Warri traffic. Kay sighed as she saw a man unzip and piss on a wall by the side of the road.

The Mercedes slowed down on the poorly constructed bridge built of bricks. They drove past a group of bare-chested children. The Mercedes got stuck on the sandy road just before Mama Afoke's family house. Ejiro hit the accelerator hard and managed to spin the car tyres out of the sand. They found the bungalow among a group of mud houses with rusted zinc roofs. A catholic priest conducted the funeral service as Mama Afoke's body lay in a coffin. Ejiro and Kay were surprised at the big population in attendance. A young girl of about six led them to a row where they easily found empty seats.

'Mama Afoke is undoubtedly with our Lord Jesus Christ,' the priest said. 'She died knowing that her children will live a good life because she brought them up in the fear of God. Mama Afoke struggled to send her first daughter to the polytechnic in Auchi. She also struggled to send her son to the University of Benin. She was determined and focused. She is what I can confidently refer to as a real African mother. In spite of being a widow at twenty-five, she chose not to remarry. She chose to focus on raising her children properly to become responsible adults.'

Ejiro looked at Kay and said, 'Let me show you around the village.'

'Promise me you will say nothing about the financial support we gave her and her children,' Kay pleaded.

Ejiro showed Kay the stream the village was named after. Some children bathed and swam in it. A kilometre away from the stream, Ejiro pointed at a brown bungalow, 'That's my grandparents' house.'

'Let's go and see them,' Kay suggested.

'We can't. They are no different from my parents. They were supposed to be at the funeral. They probably decided not to attend because of Mama Afoke's connection to us,' Ejiro said and led Kay toward the village market, where everybody stared at them. They returned to Mama Afoke's family house and met a queue of friends and relatives who took turns to have one final look at Mama Afoke's body. They joined the line.

The body, dressed in traditional Urhobo attire with a *gele* wrapped on her head, appeared slimmer. A woman in the crowd started to cry.

Night soon came and both women settled in a bedroom Greg provided for them. Ejiro could not sleep; Kay wept before she slept and this kept Ejiro awake. Mama Afoke's face kept appearing in her mind and she imagined how her aunt had described lesbianism to the village people.

Someone knocked on the door and Ejiro went to check. Uncle Greg smiled behind the door. She followed him to the courtyard where they both sat on a bench.

'I was unsure if you were still awake,' he said. 'I am sorry I have been busy. Most of the people who came from outside the village depend on me for transportation and accommodation.'

'That isn't fair. Well, I am glad you came because I couldn't sleep. I didn't see you at the burial.

'I was there briefly. My wife's cousin also passed away and I went to see his family.'

'So many deaths.'

Her uncle stood up to fetch some groundnuts from a sack lying by the wall. He gave her some. He tossed them into his mouth and said, 'You have really made up your mind about Kay?'

'How else can I be happy? I am just glad you are here – you are the only supportive relation I have.'

'I see that your parents are still keeping their distance.'

'Yes o. They all are. Uncle Mike, Brother Ike . . . And even Grandpapa and Grandmama.'

'You cannot blame them.'

'Uncle Greg, if you didn't live in the west I bet you will be like them.'

'There are many Nigerians in the diaspora that would rather die than have a lesbian daughter. I think my rejection of religion is what allows me to accept people as they are. In Sweden, gay relationships have blended so well into the society but I still have my personal reservations.' He got up and went toward some sugarcane beside the sack of groundnuts. He took a stick and used a knife to cut himself a sizeable piece. He brought it back with him and began peeling. 'Ejiro George, you have never asked me of my opinion on gay relationships, have you?'

'But you have always been excited about me and Kay.'

'Yes, of course. But let me tell you this. I never supported the legalisation for gay marriage in Sweden. I remember having a brawl on the subject with my supervisor when I was rounding up my doctorate.'

'You stand against same-sex marriage, Uncle Greg?'

'I stand against injustice.' He nodded his head. 'Let me tell you a story. Two blocks away from the flat I used to live in Stockholm, there was this man called Devin whose wife passed away and left behind a twelve-year-old daughter. You know what he did? He began to abuse his little girl. He made his own daughter his sex-slave. The Swedish police got to know about this ten years later. The poor daughter already had two children from her father. She loved her father and didn't let him stay a week in jail. She claimed their sex was consensual. After same-sex marriage became legitimate in Sweden, the girl, Rosa, who was separated from her father, filed a petition requesting for the same rights given to gay people. Ejiro, a day is coming when a woman would wed a stallion in church.' He split a peeled size of his sugarcane.

Back in bed beside Kay, Ejiro still couldn't sleep. Uncle Greg appeared to worsen her state. She wondered how a man could gain a bachelor's degree and a Ph.D. in Engineering from a

Swedish University, only to come back to Nigeria, build a house in his village and stick to petty farming. There was a rumour about his failed attempt to swindle a woman in Stockholm. When the police began investigations, he fled to Nigeria and his village become his safe haven. She found a newspaper on a shelf in the room with a story in it about the latest Nigerian pastor to buy a private jet, but realised she only stared at sentences without comprehension. Her mind wandered to London – that confused moment in a decent relationship with Olutayo, a twenty-three-year-old pastor and son of a pastor. Their ministry grew widely in the UK with Olutayo assigned to lead the branch she served in as an usher. She remembered the day she revealed her relationship with Kay to him.

'We should go on a seventy day fast,' he suggested.

'No. I can't,' she replied.

'This is a serious matter. This same sex thing is a strong bondage,' he said, narrowing his eyes.

'Olutayo, I am sorry. I wish you can understand.'

'For the sake of our relationship I will begin a fast,' he finally said.

Olutayo began his fasting that day. That same day she loosened his belt for the first time. Olutayo, known for his loud speaking in tongues, thrust himself in-between her legs ecstatically. It continued for days. He hungered for her body than he did for God. Ejiro trusted his feelings for her but she could not give him what he needed. During their intimacies, his panting was intense, and his thrusts, feeble. She got worried.

On their last night together, her faith in religion ended. He turned cold and still beside her. She shook his body but he failed to respond. She dialled his father's number and then 999. She didn't realise how naked she was until the police came. The police found some clothes for her before Olutayo's father and some other junior pastors walked in.

In the days ahead, she visited the police station several times. Since she hadn't stabbed Olutayo or shot him, the judge referred her to a psychologist. Her psychologist fed her books on recovery; it took half a year for her to finish them. Her last therapy was to face Olutayo's father. She sat in the reception and waited for twenty minutes before the door to his office opened. She couldn't imagine his reaction.

She said all she wanted to say, spoke of her bisexuality and of his son's dry fast.

It took four minutes of ghostly silence for him to talk.

'You are a serpent that will perish in hell,' he said.

He stood up, straightened his black suit and hesitantly approached her. He struck her on the face with the back of his hand. A tear rolled down her cheek. She expected more, and he struck her repeatedly. She cried and let him spit on her as her nose bled. He kicked her and lamented about the pain she caused him, his wife and his ministry.

She left the building with a swollen eye and bleeding lips, drove to Kay's Neasden apartment and banged on the door. Kay came out, her mouth agape, shocked. They hugged. A kind of heat enveloped Ejiro's body. She felt feverish and her growing headache caused her to hate life.

'What time do we leave for Warri?' Kay, who sat at the edge of the bed with a make-up box on her lap, asked.

The question jarred Ejiro from the memories of UK. 'We should leave as soon as we can. I couldn't sleep much. You will drive us.'

18.

Tito switched on the light in his bedroom. The voices of the women whose blood were on his hands reminded him of his filthiness. They spoke about the bisexuality he carried as a secret. They called him a bloody pig, kept him awake. He was sure the staff on shift were asleep when he heard a tap on his door. Ethan was ready for the plan. He sat up in bed and held his face in his palms. He desired to enjoy this night.

This country offered him a better life regardless of his crime. His mother facilitated his immigration here so he wouldn't put her or his father to shame. The support home service was just interested in the funds he generated from taxpayers' money.

He searched the drawer beside his bed and found the body spray he bought yesterday. Singh was pleased with the choice. 'It gets rid of your body odour,' he said. The comment offended Tito but he didn't react. His silence inspired Singh to write a good progress report for the day. Tito opened the door. Ethan wasn't there. He turned around and looked at his room. If all went well, it would be goodbye to the blue duvet, the small fan, the television and the clothes in the wardrobe.

Tito walked to Ethan's door, pushed it open and entered.

'I have been waiting for you,' Ethan whispered.

'I told you I would be here at three o'clock,' Tito replied and looked at the clock in the room.

'It's four-thirty,' said Ethan.

'Oh.' Tito hated clocks. The shadow of the windowpane on Ethan's neatly made bed moved due to the slight breeze outside. He was surprised Ethan took time to make his bed regardless of the plan. 'It's going to be a long night.'

'I am too excited, Tito! I would like to see how it goes,' Ethan said.

'Shhh . . . What's that sound?' Tito asked, tiptoeing to the bathroom. Ethan followed. Water dripped slowly and consistently into the sink.

'You have to turn off your tap properly.'

Ethan walked past Tito, entered his bathroom and tightened the tap. Tito sat on the bed.

'You are messing up my bed,' said Ethan.

'Why do you have to care about it? Everything is going to be on fire.'

A glint showed on Ethan's face. 'Yes! We are setting the world on fire.' He was going to grasp a freedom unknown to the imagination.

Tito stood up and began pacing in the room. He switched off the light. The light in Ethan's bathroom streamed in. He stood in front of the only curtain in the room and pulled it to the side. Auckland loomed in the landscape. He saw dots of lights from different residential buildings. A bird chirped.

'Where is the lighter?' he asked.

Ethan ransacked his clothes in the wardrobe in search of the lighter. His hands trembled as he gave the lighter to Tito. It fell. Tito picked it up.

Tito turned his back on Ethan and drew the curtain to cover the window.

'Are you ready?' Tito asked.

'Yes,' Ethan nodded.

'Light it,' Tito said, handing the lighter back.

Ethan became a bit frightened as he lifted the lighter. Tito took out the body spray from his pocket. Ethan lit the lighter.

'Ready?'

Ethan nodded.

Tito let the body spray with sketchy designs flush over the flame. The fire blazed at Ethan's fear and excitement, and caught the curtain. Tito cut off the pressure on the spray. Ethan let the lighter fall. And they both watched the fire climb up to the ceiling.

The heat from the growing fire circulated. Both boys ran downstairs. Tito imagined staff Singh, Andrew and Gus dying in their sleep. He wished the other patients Tony and Frankie, dead, too. He kicked the door downstairs open and they went out. He anticipated watching the house burn. Ethan mimicked his pleasure. And he smiled watching smoke rise into the sky. The alarm went off and his smile vanished. At the first sign of fire, Singh sprang up. At the other end of the building, Andrew jumped through the window. Gus, Tony and Frankie followed.

'Someone call 111!' Gus screamed.

'I did already,' Singh shouted. His eyes red with sleep.

The fire blazed in the upper part of the building where Tito's room, Ethan's and the office were.

The emergency lights of fire fighters shone from afar.

'What the hell caused the fire?' Andrew said into the smoky atmosphere.

As everyone stared at Tito, his eyes fell on Ethan.

19.

Michael opened his eyes and realised he was on the floor. He raised his head and looked around. He lay on the floor in front of a congregation. Shit! What was he doing lying on the floor? He sprang up and shamefully avoided the people's eyes. He walked toward the seat seven rows away where he remembered he sat. A camera trailed him. He wished he could grab the camera and smash it on the floor. Rayleigh had warned him.

'Hello, sir,' the pastor in front spoke into the microphone.

Hell, no! The preacher looked in his direction. Michael stared at the massive screen in front of the congregation and saw himself in it.

'Are you talking to me?' Michael asked.

A young woman rushed to him and shoved a microphone toward his lips.

'Can you come back, please?' the pastor said.

Michael nodded in disappointment and headed back. He felt light walking back to the altar. 'What is going on?' he asked.

'Can you remember what you said a few minutes ago?' the pastor replied.

‘I did not say anything,’ Michael replied and heard laughter erupt in the congregation.

‘Young man, you said your mission is to destroy the body you live in.’

‘Is there any sense in what you are saying?’ Michael replied.

The laughter rose.

‘You have been delivered from the evil spirit tormenting you,’ the pastor said. ‘Go back to your seat.’

He didn’t hear a word of the sermon preached afterwards. He kept wondering what had happened. He couldn’t have been lying dead on the floor. He wasn’t drunk – how could he have said what the pastor claimed? He remembered a certain young woman claiming to be the spirit of masturbation before his consciousness went blank. This disturbed him.

After the service, he talked with the man sitting beside him but he couldn’t comprehend the man’s words. He couldn't have crawled over the floor like a toddler and threatened the pastor. He couldn’t have claimed to be a demon except if the tea they forced him to drink at the beginning of the service had something in it that made him lose his mind. He stood to his feet and shook with fury.

'It wasn't you speaking but the spirit living inside you,' the man repeated.

'Absurd . . . I really need to go.'

On his way back to his Lagos apartment, he imagined himself, repeatedly, in front of the congregation. It couldn't be him. The busy traffic gave him time to ruminate. In the rear view mirror of the taxi, he saw an overheated van smoking. Commuters stepped out of taxis to hop on okadas, whose riders, in a hazardous but competent way undoubtedly surmounted the hold-up.

He rang Rayleigh and told her about his experience. She laughed uncontrollably.

'Too funny to be true, Michael.'

'I suspect foul play. I suspect that tea they gave me.'

'Church is serious business in Africa. Anything for money,' she said.

20.

Someone asked to see Rayleigh in the lobby. She perceived the person to be the caller whose calls she missed.

'Madam, it's the Minister of . . .'

'Gosh! Tell him I am not in Nigeria for a religious visit,' Rayleigh replied before the young woman finished speaking.

'Please, Madam, hear me out nah.'

Rayleigh stared at the worried receptionist in the blue and white outfit that all the hotel staff wore. She looked anxious. It occurred to Rayleigh that the visitor might not be the preacher she met in the lobby. That preacher almost ruined the excitement that James's email brought her earlier in the day. She nodded at the woman.

'You need to come down, Madam.'

'Who is he?'

'Our Minister of Information, Madam,' the woman replied, pronouncing the word, 'our' with reverence.

'Give me a moment.' Rayleigh closed the door and rested her back on it. She sighed and approached the mirror. She stared at her image and coloured her lips. She found her phone and dialled Chioma's number.

'Hi, Ray! Aren't you supposed to be having a meeting with the minister?'

'How did you know this, Chioma?'

'There is no access into the hotel right now. I am standing out here and waiting.'

Rayleigh ran her fingers through her hair. 'I will see you later then. I really don't know what he wants.'

In the lobby, two policemen approached her and led her to the bar. The minister wore a white caftan. A red tube floated in the pool before them.

A policeman offered her a seat. She sat and crossed her legs.

'Miss Johnson, the nation sympathises with you. The culprits will be brought to justice,' the minister said, his eyes fixed on her for a moment. He glanced at the policeman that offered her a seat. 'Please, meet the Police Inspector General, Aliyu Yusuf.'

'Hello, Inspector General.' She forced a smile.

'Nice to meet you, Madam. Your loss is our loss. The police will support you and your team,' he said.

She glanced at the minister's large belly. It rose and fell while he spoke. The clean-shaven minister spoke in an imitated British accent.

'We know it is impossible for any compensation to replace loss,' he said, as he took out a brown envelope and gave it to Rayleigh. 'Please, take this as a token.'

She received it and pressed it against her chest. It felt like a gift from her late sister.

'Those militants who claim they are fighting for their land are nuts. They put the blame on the government for the illiteracy they inflict on themselves. They put the blame on all white people, thinking they own the Shell or Mobil companies,' the police chief said. 'They have a hand in your loss, Madam. We will surely bring them to face justice.'

* * *

Chioma walked into the lobby.

In quick strides, Rayleigh led the way to her room. She pushed the door open and slouched on the chair. 'Nigeria never ceases to amaze me.'

'How much did he give?' Chioma asked, her eyes on the brown envelope.

Rayleigh reached for it with reluctance and tore it open, removed a cheque in it and was dumbfounded for a minute. 'What am I to do with this?'

Chioma took the cheque and glared at it. 'I can't believe this.'

'They have made me rich.'

'Yes, Rayleigh,' Chioma said and dropped the cheque. 'They are trying to distract you from the truth.'

Rayleigh narrowed her eyes.

'The militants had nothing to do with Kay's death. Tito was never part of them.'

'How do you know that?'

Chioma opened her handbag and brought out a folded newspaper page, which she gave to Rayleigh. 'Read this.'

Rayleigh read it silently.

'It isn't advisable to seek a rogue declared wanted,' Chioma warned.

'By whom? By the police or the government, who, themselves, are rogues? We are supposed to be journalists, Chioma,' Rayleigh replied. 'I need the truth.'

'In Afghanistan, bodies of journalists can be found in shreds. In North Korea, bodies of foreign journalists are dumped on the borders. But here in Nigeria, it would be a miracle if a journalist's body is found at all.'

'Don't scare me, Chioma. I think I need a drink.'

Both women decided to visit the hotel bar.

The bar had a few customers. The music of Fela Kuti reverberated within it.

'I think we should get a bottle of whiskey and share,' Rayleigh said.

'I don't do spirits. You can order what you like. I will take beer.'

'If I had been listening to you, I would be nowhere. You know that?' Rayleigh said.

'Have you heard of occultism before?' Chioma asked.

'Voodoo or . . . a kind of spirituality, I guess,' Rayleigh replied.

'The militants you want to speak to are occultists.'

* * *

She turned around and saw a black car approach in a swirl of dust.

Two men in masked faces emerged from the car. They wore camouflage and black trousers tucked into boots. They caught her after she gained four long strides and dragged her into the car. Someone's palms covered her face – she struggled for breath and couldn't scream. As the car sped off, she kicked against the seats and attempted to wriggle her hands out of a man's fists behind her. The car's narrow interior didn't let her fight for long.

The car slowed down in a quiet but populated area. She met the gazes of people who ignored what they saw – a white woman with a seal over her mouth sitting between two masked faces in a car. A woman, in front of a food store, screamed at her children for staring at the car.

Rayleigh tried to mumble.

'Quiet, abeg!' one of the men said in a deep and drawling voice.

They covered her face with a rag that stunk of perspiration. She felt a headache and became unconscious.

She woke, and could smell the foliage; she was alone in an abandoned hall with windows slightly opened and plants peeping in. Her hands were bound behind her back. Her breath stank and she felt a foul taste in her mouth. She tried to get up to her feet but her ankles ached. Her spine too. She sat up instead, and felt relieved. She acquainted herself with the concrete floor, the stained white ceiling and the snaky grasses making their way into the room through the windows. A tall, slim man walked in, trailed by three other men. He didn't cover his face like the three men behind him.

'You are awake now, honey,' he said.

'What do you want?' she asked, wriggling her body.

'*She fine, no be small*,' one of the masked men said. And they laughed at her.

'What do you want from me?' she demanded in a calmer tone.

'The question surprises me. Should it not be – what do you want from us?' the unmasked man answered.

She noticed his dimples.

He gestured at the other men to leave.

'Who are you?' she asked when the others left.

'I am your true lover whom you have been searching for.'

'What you are talking about?'

He sighed and sat beside her. 'From the first day a government spokesman poisoned your heart against my movement, you started a search for me. The walls have ears. I know everything. My father started the movement I now run. He died for it.' He brought out a knife. She trembled. He reached behind her and she closed her eyes. He swiped the knife twice. The rope on her hands fell apart.

She sighed, rubbed her liberated palms in front of her face and massaged her knuckles.

He looked away from her. 'We are fighting for the land, the oil, and for Niger-Delta people. The federal government and foreign investors have been depriving us of what is rightfully ours for a long time. We own the oil of Nigeria, yet we have the worst roads compared to the rest of the country. Countless accidents yearly. We kidnap foreigners who cooperate with the government in raping us and stealing our oil. We have no reason to have you here.'

'You are a lying pig. Did my sister have anything to do with your oil?'

He turned around and caught her stare. Something stirred inside her. She stood up and walked to one of the open windows.

'If I had anything to do with her death, you wouldn't be here alive, English girl.'

She ran toward and pounded him on his chest, helplessly, with her fists. He pushed her and she fell to the concrete floor.

'I have slit throats. I have tasted blood. For greed. For justice. For hate. For good. For revenge. I wouldn't hesitate to kill you if you cross my boundary.'

She listened with a confused glare and embraced his slow words.

He turned his back on her and wiped his face with his fingers. The edge of his knife stuck out of the knife-holder buckled to his side. Tears flowed on her cheeks. The creeping plants in the window swayed to a slight breeze.

'I don't blame them. I don't people who see me as a criminal. I am a good soldier now. I do not say these words to give you a good image of myself or prove you wrong. I already have an ugly image. I had my men bring you here, so I could personally ask you to shut the hell up and go after the real killer.'

She nodded. 'I have heard you.'

'The government blame us for your sister's death. I did not murder her and none of my men are involved.'

'What is your story then?' she asked.

The smell of vegetation wafted in the air. He squatted before her, so close that his breath that smelled like bandage over a wound, hit her face.

.

'I fight for Niger-Delta,' he began. 'For my people, the land. All Nigerians depend on oil, but are blind to the suffering of the people that live in the region where the oil comes from. I watched my father form this great movement. But Nigeria murdered him and thought it had killed our cause. But my father died a hero. So will I. So will my sons.' He brought out a metallic cigarette pack and offered her a cigarette.

There was something about his eyes. Narrow. They held a grave persuasiveness.

He lit the cigarette between her lips, and she stood up.

He lit another for himself, too. The smell of fried chilli sauce came with the breeze.

She sighed and said, 'I just need you to let me go.'

'Just like that?' he replied.

She dragged on her cigarette and laughed sadly. 'Are you going demand a ransom? I have no one on earth at this moment. England wouldn't care if I rot here.'

He left the cigarette burning in his lips and folded his arms.

'Do you know who is responsible then?'

'My people have no hand in your sister's death. The government knows who is responsible. You think if I needed your money, I wouldn't demand the seventeen thousand pounds given to you by the government?'

'How do you know about that?' she asked, peering into his eyes. 'Voodoo?'

'You shouldn't be mindful of walls alone. Even the clouds could have ears. A senator in this country, who is my uncle, the father of your sister's murderer, was behind the death of my father. He betrayed his own brother because of politics. I used to know Tito. I loved him. I bought him toys when he was growing up. He was never part of us. How could he, behaving like a psycho?'

She pictured the brown envelope on the reading table in her hotel room.

One of the masked men brought in a plate of rice and a bowl of curry stew. Steam rose from the plate of rice and the pieces of meat.

'You should eat.'

She stared at her unmasked companion. He nodded his head and reached for the plate. He fetched some of the rice and ate it himself, to assure her it was safe. She collected the fork from him and fed herself.

* * *

The hunger for a cigarette woke her. She batted her eyelids. She found herself wearing a seatbelt in the same car that was used to abduct her. Beside her was the unmasked militant.

He took away a burning cigarette from his lips and tossed it through the window. They stopped in a taxi park and he pulled up by the side of the street.

'Go there and take a taxi back to your hotel.'

She unfastened the seatbelt.

'Chase the facts now.' He reached for her handbag in the back seat and dropped it on her lap. 'You might not be able to prove it but at least you know now. Get out!'

She opened the door and stepped out. He drove away. She looked at the car's plate number, forced herself against memorising it, but it stuck.

21.

Tito heard no sound and concluded Singh was asleep. He turned on the lights and saw the full image of his naked body in the mirror. He stared and lusted over himself. He opened the door and slipped into the corridor, passed by the doors that led to the laundry and the staff office. He entered the lobby, felt the wall with his palms and struggled to acquaint his eyes with the darkness. Singh lay on the couch before Hahona's door and snored loudly.

Tito walked past Singh and took a deep breath. He almost lost his footing as Singh's snoring rose.

He reached Hahona's door. Singh stopped snoring. Tito turned around slowly to check if Singh was still asleep. He started to snore again. Tito weighed down the doorknob and pushed the door. The resulting sound quietened Singh's snore briefly before readjusting to its normal rhythm. He pushed the door open, entered Hahona's room and left the door ajar. Hahona was half-awake in the dimly lit room. His eyes widened in fear when he saw Tito. Tito mounted him and worked his arousal against Hahona's groin. Hahona turned his body gently, rid his track pants, and shoved himself against Tito's groin. Tito's thrusts, like whispers, forced tears out of Hahoha's eyes. Their bodies were drenched with sweat; their breathing got intense. Tito let out a gulp of breath over Hahona and fell by his side, breathless. Tito caught Singh's figure on the doorway, then pushed himself to the floor and crawled away from the bed.

'What is happening here?' Singh asked. 'Gech out now, Tito,' he said.

Hahona's intense breathing faded. But Tito's begins, but does not bully the ambience within the room. He walked past Singh with high shoulders.

Back in his room, Tito held onto his laughter. He grabbed the duvet and pounced on the bed in delight as he felt the dampness between his thighs. What will Singh do? There is the sound of assiduous coughing outside his room.

* * *

Singh and Michael sat opposite Hahona across the brown office table. Tito was in front of Phiona, who bore the letter that was to accompany him to hell.

'I liked it I-I-want him to stick it up my arse, again,' Hahona said.

Tito thought it was funny and laughed.

Phiona looked at Singh, and Singh had his head down.

'Are you sure you weren't forced?' Phiona asked Hahona.

'I like it. Thank you. Thank you!' Hahona replied. He looked away from Phiona to Singh, and from Singh to Michael.

Phiona's stare fell on Tito. 'How long has this been going on?'

'First time. It's the first time,' Tito answered.

22.

Rayleigh stood over her sister's grave. She brought out a bottle of fragrance and sprinkled on it. The flowers and the leaves she left three days ago were gone. She paid two adolescent boys to weed the grasses growing on grave. Termites infested another grave close by. The insects boldly maintained their mansion over it. One of the hired boys claimed he heard the spirit of the dead in the termite-infested grave hiss. Rayleigh looked at the name. Eloke Sandra, 1984 – 2006.

'She hissed because she sees the weeding as a waste of time,' the other boy said.

Their words scared her. They left her alone and for a moment. On the left side of her sister's grave was another grave overgrown with grasses. The words on the tomb read: 'RIP Naked Wire'. The cross over it had a dent. She smelled marijuana and heard someone cough. Four teenage boys smoked yards away.

She remembered the day Kay was buried. Everyone who knew Kay lived in England, hence, only two persons were present: herself and Chioma. She asked to attend the burial of Kay's lover Ejiro. So a few days later, Chioma drove her to the village where the road was recently constructed with red sand and burnt bricks. The memories of the thatched roofs and rusted zinc sheets she saw were still fresh in Rayleigh's memory. The burial procession was like a festival. Many people attended it and wailed over the brown coffin. Yellow starch and banga soup, with so much pieces of meat, was served. A catholic mass followed. People stared at her; she wasn't sure if they were disgusted or curious about her presence. The children who were friendly toward her were redirected by parents.

'Why do they come here to bury her? Why not in the town's graveyard with my sister?' she had asked Chioma.

'People are buried in their place of origin,' Chioma explained. 'It is a practice in most Nigerian cultures. There's an exception though. A married woman is expected to be buried in her husband's village when she dies.'

'What about the ones buried at the graveyard in the town?'

'Their ancestors come from the town. But most of them who are buried there are not really from there. No one cared or was ready to spend enough money to have their bodies taken to their village.'

Rayleigh felt a sharp prick in her right feet. Her thoughts faded away. She bent and checked. There was little bleeding. She pulled off the shoe, took out the little rusted nail out before cleaning the blood with a handkerchief. She wore the shoe again and wiped her fingers against her jeans.

23.

A storm hovered over Sydney; the wind raised the dust and composed a little orchestra of noise. Michael Merije stayed awake since it started by four in the morning. Okafor Obi slept undisturbed. The light by the bedside cast shadows on the wall. Michael stared at the flower-shaped tattoo on Okafor's body.

Okafor inhaled heavily, stretched and opened his eyes. 'Why up so early, Mike?' he asked in a feeble voice.

'We need to talk, cobber,' Michael said quietly.

Michael got up from the bed; his shadow faded from the wall and left Okafor's behind.

'What's the matter?' Okafor asked.

'Who is Sue Chong-Xuzin?' Michael replied and began to pace within the room.

Okafor raised a brow and gradually brought down his feet to the tiled floor. He stared at his own nakedness, walked toward the window and stared into the dark.

'Answer me, Okafor.'

Okafor covered his face and hissed. He ignored Michael and entered the bathroom. In the shower, he washed away his growing fear and pain. His eleven months affair with Michael, all he had, was now ending. He remembered Sue and that first day she said yes to him. He remembered her fingers on his body and her quick pace by the seaside. It was their last time together. She flew out of Singapore that night.

For the uncountable time in a year, he re-imagined what happened at Narita Airport in March 2009. She didn't know about the drugs. The happy young woman was confronted by Japanese Customs and she excitedly told them of her intended holiday in Tokyo. When kilos of cannabis were found in her luggage, she fainted. Her tears did not stop the Customs officers from detaining her.

Still in the shower, Okafor knew his game was over. He would leave Australia. Michael would not write the letter required for him to extend his stay in the country. He remembered how he met Michael online: the Skype calls and Facebook chats that reduced the distance between Australia and Singapore.

His thoughts remained in Singapore for a while as he thought of the calls from the police to his Singapore flat. First, they asked about his forsaken study at the university, and then the status of his visa. His few acquaintances in

Singapore, including his Nigerian flatmates, knew little of his status and were okay with his lies. His name was once popular in the dark boroughs through Tokyo, Bangkok, Johor and Singapore. He used to enjoy the threesomes on beds littered with US dollars and remnants of cannabis.

He came out of the bathroom with a towel over his shoulders. Michael stood, his back against the wall. 'O boy, are you going to call the police now?' Okafor asked.

'You planned to use me next, I reckon?' Michael answered.

'I see you have really done your homework. Whatever I say now will not change anything. But I must tell you this. I really loved Sue. I wanted to marry her. I had her make that single trip to Tokyo so we could raise money for our lives afterwards, but they caught her. I could not do it myself because Nigerian passports attract problems all the time. She had a Singaporean passport and would not be much headache passing through Customs. I swear I did not come after you because you had an Australian passport. I had no intention of using you.'

Michael had heard how Nigerian scammers made a good life by ruining good people. But it never caused him to suspect Okafor.

Okafor sorted his clothes from the wardrobe.

Michael wanted to ask Okafor if their relationship meant anything to him. Or why he delighted in spoiling his country's name. Instead went to Okafor and embraced him.

Before noon Okafor left with his luggage.

24.

Rayleigh saw as the security men around glared at her. She walked self-consciously into the government building. It had taken the minister three weeks to approve this meeting.

The minister saw her from his window enter the reception, and he told his secretary to keep her waiting so that she can have a taste of how difficult it was to see important persons in Nigeria. He asked for coffee and fidgeted with the TV's remote for a while before the screen on the wall came on.

Rayleigh sat cross-legged in the lobby and watched the television. A news update involved an emerging terrorist group in Northern Nigeria. Pictures of bombed churches followed. A reporter interviewed persons. After half an hour, the receptionist led her into the minister's office.

'It is nice to meet you, Miss Johnson,' he said, standing to his feet. 'You have come to harass an innocent servant.'

Rayleigh shook his hand and took the seat he showed her. 'I would like to know if you are ready.'

'The ball is in your court,' he answered.

She wanted to spit in his face. She turned on her recorder, placed it beside her, and started. 'I would like to know why my sister's murderer wasn't charged in court.'

'You are wrong. He was charged in court.'

'No record proves that.'

'The case was complicated. The crime was committed by a person with a psychological condition, you see. So, it is not proper that it is called a crime at all.'

'There are a lot of criminals in Nigerian prisons today whose mental conditions have never been assessed. Can't you just admit that you share an interest in this Tito you're protecting? The Minister of Information and the police chief tried to convince me that the Niger Delta militants killed my sister.'

'Not everybody is aware of the details. Miss Johnson, these things are hard. There was a court case. And the judge passed a sentence.'

'If Tito Ogheneovo was the son of an ordinary Nigerian, perhaps a bus driver, would he be enjoying life somewhere in New Zealand?'

The minister said nothing.

'And his parents wouldn't see me.'

'We have given a detailed report of the case to the British government, and it is their responsibility to explain the situation to you and any other relations of the deceased girl. The president of Nigeria takes full responsibility for the tragedy and has offered an apology.'

'An apology! Why are you such a liar?'

'I have three daughters older than you. None of them raises their voice at me. This is Nigeria. Behave yourself.'

He walked out of the office. She thought he went to the bathroom but the receptionist, who brought her in earlier, came in to lead her out. She was mad. Mad at her country. They did not even offer to fly her sister's body home.

'But he didn't say he was leaving.'

'He is on his way right now to a meeting,' the receptionist replied.

She felt tied to the green leather sofa on which she sat on.

A policeman joined the receptionist at the door. She stood up and turned off her recorder. As she walked out of the office, the receptionist and the policeman stood aside and she passed in-between them.

'Can I give you a lift?' the policeman asked. 'I saw you come in a taxi.'

'No, thank you,' she replied.

She entered a passage and walked past two doors, not sure of where she was going.

'Over here.' The policeman re-emerged. He stood, slightly bent to his right side. He held the door behind him open.

'Thank you,' she said, and went through.

He mumbled.

She heard him, paused herself and looked at him. He had mumbled the name of her sister's killer. He looked thin and unkempt. She remembered the policemen that stopped her taxi at the airport road and demanded she pay them an entrustment fee, something she could not understand. She followed him and he led her into the car park and opened the passenger's door of a Peugeot 504 for her.

The policeman picked up the biscuit packs and banana peels that littered the passenger's seat. He gathered some papers on the foot mat and threw them in the back seat of his Peugeot. He brought a piece of cloth under the driver's seat and wiped the seat before she got in. The car stank of grease and banana.

He eased the car carefully onto the road.

'Tell me what you know,' she said.

'Madam, if I didn't say his name, you wouldn't have accepted this ride?'

'I think you know the reply to that,' she said.

He shook his head. 'I am wearing this uniform, Madam, but I don't stand for the corrupt system. If I am corrupt, poverty caused it. Poverty is the reason we policemen extort money from drivers on highways. I tell you the truth – that court case was the most surprising one I have been to in my life. That boy, Tito. I still remember his face so well.' He paused as he approached a roundabout and took the second exit.

'I stay in Shear Hills Hotel, not far fro—'

'I know Shear Hills,' he said.

She nodded, and smiled faintly.

'Tito was fascinated with the buttocks of the policewoman who led him into the courtroom. He even asked her what she was like in bed. No one could say anything because he was the son of a senator. He smiled at every question and asked the judge to read his Bible and decide for himself if lesbianism was okay. As far as I am concerned, Madam, no trial took place. You mustn't quote me. I never told you this. I found his sentence interesting. It was like sentencing a criminal to heaven. I do not support anything gay but what I saw that day kept me thinking for days. How can you send a murderer overseas for killing two people?'

She swallowed the information with difficulty.

'Thank you,' she muttered and stepped out when they got to her hotel.

'Madam, I hope you won't be mad if I request something small from you. I risked leaving my station to help you.'

She looked into his eyes, opened her handbag and gave him some change.

25.

Tito was silent all the while Jeff and Jimmy laughed and when the coordinator Lorraine spoke in her didactic voice.

He coughed.

'Tito, are you alright,' Lorraine asked.

Tito coughed again. H looked at Lorraine. She was dressed in a red suit and her hair dyed black. His eyes searched her hips and he felt a stirring between his thighs.

'I am alright,' he said. He felt something crawl in his stomach and he stood. He walked away from the circle. Lorraine stared.

'Tito, where are you going?'

'Toilet,' he replied.

He limped on his bad leg.

Lorraine watched him raise his deformed arm against the wall to support his body before he opened the door to the toilet. Tito, once handsome and unpredictable, now lived in a damaged body. His cheeks and his chin were severely scarred. A part of her desired to stop calling him Tito; he wasn't the 'Tito' she knew.

'Jimmy, let's hear from you,' she said to get Tito off her mind.

'I have got nothing to say,' twenty-three-year-old Jimmy replied, shaking his head.

'Jimmy, how can you say you have nothing to say?' Lorraine asked. 'What happened to the agreement you signed? During the last meeting, we agreed that you would welcome the woman, didn't we?'

'I am not here to screw harlots,' Jimmy replied.

Jeff squealed.

Lorraine glanced at Jeff before staring back at Jimmy. 'You are with us because you need help. How many times do we need to remind you, Jimmy? The reason you are with us is because you need help. You have abused a child in the past, which isn't appropriate, and we are trying everything possible to help you.'

'But I don't want the woman. I don't like her,' Jimmy replied.

'We can have another one to replace her.'

'No. I'm not interested.'

She shook her head. 'How do you deal with your urges when they come?'

'I just deal with them,' he replied.

'How often do you masturbate a day, Jimmy?'

Jimmy shook his head. 'I don't know.'

'Can I tell your care manager then to cancel the contract with the woman?'

He shook his head.

She scribbled down a few words on her notepad.

'Over to you, Jeff. You spoke to your care manager about getting the *Hot Rod* magazine last week. Do you understand that this magazine is meant for you and no one else?'

'Yes,' Jeff replied, shaking his broad shoulders.

'Make sure you keep it away from your flatmates.'

A strong smell entered the hall.

'Damn it! Tito will kill us!' Jeff said, his palms over his nose. They heard the sound of the toilet flushing.

'Damn it!' Tito yelled, still in the toilet. He looked into the dirtied toilet and spat. He waited for water to fill the cistern before he flushed again. He felt movement in his belly, so he sat on the toilet again. He felt so full with nothing to pass out other than the condensed smell. He stood up and grabbed the toilet roll one more time.

Outside, he met an empty hall. He walked toward the entrance and sighted Lorraine and the others outside. Jeff laughed, squatted and held his belly. Jimmy paced between Lorraine and the hall.

Tito met them. Their eyes settled on him.

'Tito, you are sick,' Lorraine said. 'You must go back. Your support staff will contact the care manager. What did you eat before coming here?'

'Rotten eggs. The smell has poisoned us,' Jimmy mumbled, still pacing.

'I didn't ask you,' Lorraine said, with a fixed gaze on Jimmy. She turned to meet Tito's gaze. 'Your support staff will take you back now.'

Michael emerged from the building. Tito stepped into the van without a word. Michael got in beside him, turned on the ignition and put the van in reverse. Lorraine waved. Jeff waved and smiled.

'What's the issue with your stomach, man?' Michael asked, as the van turned onto the road.

'It was the milk in the fridge.'

'I have told you over and over to use the powdered milk. Condensed milk isn't good for everyone. I hope you don't fart in here.'

Michael gave way to an oncoming cyclist and made a turn. He stopped, checked his blindside before he entered the motorway.

Tito sighed and scratched the hard skin on his chin. 'I should be the one determining whether I am sick or not. Not bloody Lorraine.'

'Stop using such language.'

'We need to go back, Michael. I am not sick.'

'Don't make me laugh.'

'Damn you!' Tito screamed, hitting the dashboard with his fist.

Michael sighed.

'Take the next exit and head back to Epsom or I will get out of this crap of a van.'

Michael nodded and stepped harder on the accelerator. 'Do your worst, Tito,' he said.

Tito opened the van's door and leaped. A tortuous sound on the asphalt followed. Michael applied the brakes and pulled up. Vehicles on the highway rammed into each other before Tito's unmoving body. Michael came out of the van and headed toward Tito. A driver jumped out of a truck hastily and helped Michael carry Tito's bloodied body to the side.

Michael placed his ear over Tito's heart pulsing under the bloodstained cardigan. He asked the truck driver to dial 111. Incoming cars manoeuvred around the vehicles that had stopped.

'How the hell did he jump out of the van?' someone shouted.

Michael looked away. Tito's body was a spattered exoskeleton. His torn lips remained apart and his mouth was covered with the blood. Michael placed his towel over a deep wound on Tito's skull and avoided the graphic sight entirely. He resolved to resign from his job.

A slightly built woman emerged out of the growing circle of people with a first aid box and squatted beside Michael.

26.

Chioma walked past the white desk toward the elevator. The receptionist didn't look up. She used the elevator and climbed to the fourth floor where Rayleigh's hotel room was. Rayleigh opened the door. The tiled floor was styled with flower patterns.

'This is your most important day in Nigeria,' Chioma said and sat on the sofa.

'I miss her. I miss my sister, Kay,' Rayleigh's voice almost broke. 'How was the screening? I know you have seen bits before today, but could you tell anything different?'

'You have made an exceptional film.'

'I came back to meet an email aimed at ruining my day. It was from an ex-tutor from my writing school. The witch thinks my writing is still useless.'

'Don't tell me you believe her,' Chioma said.

'I stopped working on the manuscript and posted it to my London address.'

'You shouldn't have done that.'

Silence.

'Do you have a man, Chioma?'

'No, Rayleigh. Still hopeful. I have had brief relationships with wild animals that saw themselves as men.'

Rayleigh gave a short laugh. 'I know what you are talking about. I have had some men in my life, too. Michael was different. I wanted him but he never gave me an answer.'

'Did you really ask him out?'

'I gave him clues. I thought we'd see after the screening, but he walked out when people came to hug me. It appeared like I offended him.' She gave her phone to Chioma. 'Check how many times I've called him.'

'Let us go out and have dinner, Rayleigh. You will tell me everything.'

'We have the entire night, Nigerian woman, to eat and talk.'

They used the staircase to the first floor and talked loudly. Rayleigh led the way, fidgeting with an umbrella.

27.

In the plane were the loud voices and the distressed complaints of people gripped by impatience. Michael's tired eyes roamed. An Indian girl smiled forcefully at a man who was about to take the seat beside her. A large Chinese woman struggled down the aisle and approached Michael's row. She slumped on the seat beside him. Another woman, in front, before the business class section, nearly dropped her toddler. The baby whined.

The plane took off fifteen minutes later out of Lagos. He looked down over Lagos; the elevations coloured by dry and green vegetation, the blue colour of the Atlantic Ocean. The plane slipped over a rolling ball of cloud. He looked away from the window to the woman who sat beside him; she had touched him for support. 'Why can't the pilot stop the plane from shaking?' she complained, not exactly to him. He smiled and looked away.

He declined the late dinner. The woman beside him requested juice, a sandwich and carrot cake.

'You are sure you want nothing, sir?' the flight attendant asked him, narrowing her eyes.

'Nothing,' he said under his breath.

The attendant wore a necklace he looked at a second time. She reminded him of the night he spent on Rayleigh's bed.

'It's so funny all we do is lay on the bed, stare at each other lustfully and do nothing but talk,' Rayleigh said, resting her head on his chest, her pyjamas top barely covering her breasts.

He played with her hair. 'You know I can't. I have feelings. But I cannot place you under the category of women I have had in the past.'

'Who cares? I have everything a slut has.'

'Stop it, Rayleigh.'

She lit her cigarette.

He sighed.

'Don't worry. I won't spill ash on you.'

'Worried about tomorrow?'

'I don't know. It seems my sister die again tomorrow. I don't know if you understand. But you see, I have been in Nigeria putting everything into the documentary and my writing project that I am still unsure of. Writing, investigating, travelling and filming have all been about me since I entered this country. The film revealed more than I expected. There are still some unanswered questions, Michael.'

'Questions.'

'Yes. Essential and non-essential questions.'

'I presume I can help out with the non-essential questions,' Michael said.

'What does the name, Tito, mean? The Nigerians I have spoken to say it has no meaning. They aren't even sure if the name is Nigerian.'

Michael laughed. 'I know the origin of the name.'

'Really?'

'Tito was named Christopher. His father rather called him Christo. When he started school, his teacher couldn't pronounce the name, Christo. The teacher pronounced Christo as Tito. And everyone in school started calling him that. The name remained. Christo faded away.'

'Thanks Michael.' Halfway with the cigarette, she put it out, turned over and looked into his eyes. 'I am not sure of your desires. Sometimes I think you want me and sometimes . . .' she stopped.

He knew his desires were quiet and persistent but found it difficult to admit it to her. 'Don't start this, again,' he said.

'Do you know that no racist would ever admit being a racist?' she asked.

'Why do you bring that up?'

'Because I think I am one. Even if my body desires you, I remain the beast that I am, having a thing against Africans as my sister once spoke of me. No one knew me as she did. The first day she accused me I felt bad. I didn't really like her partner, Ejiro.'

'Are you trying to say something?' Michael asked.

She laughed. 'Do you think I am a racist?'

'I never said that.'

'Will you help me mother a baby?'

He adjusted himself quietly to a sitting position. His eyes searched her body. 'Now a racist woman wants a black child,' he teased her.

'Michael, I'm serious.'

He laughed and lay back on the bed. He closed his eyes and said, 'But there are so many dudes here in Nigeria. So many attractive men . . .'

'It is you I want, Michael.'

'I am not that straight.'

'I don't care.'

'Are you asking for this so I will make love to you?'

Her eyes fluttered 'Never mind,' she said.

Now in the plane heading for Sydney, he blamed himself for being around her for too long.

He closed the door to her hotel room and left for his apartment. He felt afraid she might never want to see him again.

'What a nice feeling to have left me with, Michael,' she said on the phone.

'Ray . . .'

'The night was so good. You made it so pleasant. You made me feel eighteen again, Michael.'

'Rayleigh, please, forgive me.'

'You have made me realise something about myself. Never mind anyway. I am no longer interested in you.'

'I know,' he said. 'I see you have been drinking.'

'I want a child, Michael. Please, just tell me you will think about it.'

'Rayleigh, you should be thinking of the screening.'

'I didn't come all the way here to screen or make a film. I came to find out the truth, and re-establish a connection with my sister. And I have done that.'

'Okay-okay. I will think about it.'

'I would expect an answer after the screening,' she said and hung up.

He stared at his phone and wondered.

The plane arrived Doha. Michael joined a queue and checked in for the next flight to Sydney. He sat in one of the lounges with some Nigerian sportswomen in green and white outfit.

One of them asked him if he had come from Nigeria.

'Yes. I got on the six o'clock flight from Lagos this morning.'

The women exchanged stares.

'Really?' The tallest among them, with no hair on her scalp, probed him.

'I was born in Australia. Lived almost all my life in Sydney.'

'Your pronunciation of Lah-gos gave you away. It is Lagos. *Ley-gos*,' a light complexioned woman among them, stressed. He joined them and laughed about it.

They were footballers going for a tournament in Hong Kong. They made him promise he'd watch them play against Canada in two weeks. He soon headed toward the departure gate.

This time in the plane bound for Sydney, he sat next to an Indian man in his late sixties. He barely noticed the take-off due to his fatigue.

His thoughts went back to his last moments in Lagos. He felt uncomfortable with the prolonged applause. He wondered if Nigerians should applaud Rayleigh's work or sympathise with her over Kay's death. They all knew the killer was the son of influential people in government. As Rayleigh received an ovation from the audience, she wept silently beside him. A minister had flown in from Abuja to watch the screening; but few senators were present. He couldn't stay and watch, lest he gripped someone by the throat. Nigeria had puked on his face. On her face. And he left her as shook hands and hugged attendants at the screening. His answer to her was going be 'yes'. He wanted to tell her he could help her bring a child into the world. But he needed to run, to be away from anything affiliated with Tito, which Rayleigh re-enacted in her film, as he recalled Tito's bloodied frame that unholy day by the side of the road.

* * *

They all got off the plane in a single file and a black, hairy dog under the control of an immigration officer sniffed passenger's pants and shoes.

The dog sniffed Michael's shoes, moved on briefly and turned around. It whined and jumped, shaking its controller's grasp. The officer asked Michael to follow her.

'What have you got on you?' she asked, scanning his passport.

'Just myself and my damn luggage filled with clothes.'

'Why did the dog react that way?' she asked.

'You guys did well by not picking me yourselves this time. I think your dog needs to be schooled, too.'

The woman gave him his passport after copying some details, she showed him to the section where he'd claim his luggage. After getting his luggage, an officer led him into an office and asked him if he smoked marijuana.

He was the only passenger whose clothes and books were taken out of his luggage, whose pockets were turned out, whose privacy on the pages of his diary was violated.

'You can go now. You have to understand we do this for security reasons.'

'Do your job well and stop embarrassing black people,' he replied.

The Caucasian officer quietly helped Michael arrange his few books and clothes into the bag. He zipped up the bag and murmured, 'Have a good day.'

It rained while an Aboriginal song played in the train. The song soon died away and an announcement followed:

THIS IS MASCOT.

(After two minutes): DOORS CLOSING.

THE NEXT DESTINATION IS GREEN SQUARE.

He knew these words well. His boyhood memories returned to him when the train arrived at Hornsby station. He wondered what Ash looked like these days under that thatch of blonde hair. Nine years ago, he invited him to his house to meet his parents. The sun's flaky rays snuck in through spaces between the curtains. His father tried, fruitlessly, to convince Ash on what a penis was.

'This ugly meaty part of a man's body is for a woman, used to bear children, and by a man to gain dignity.'

Michael never forgot that day. Ash vanished from his life thereafter.

Nothing changed on the street he once lived in. He remembered the rustling sound from the railroad behind their three-bedroom house, and the noises of schoolchildren in the school blocks away. The wooden fence around the house, which used to be brown, now had a white colour. The lawn his father mowed fortnightly remained unchanged. The wooden door painted a silver colour with a transparent glass frame in its upper part. An emerald green lace revealed itself from inside. He knocked and checked his watch. His parents could be at work. Damn academics. He walked across the road to the liquor store, bought a bottle of whiskey and returned. He sat in front of the door and opened the bottle. He wondered if they knew about his trip to Nigeria and if his mother still suffered from back pain.

* * *

They returned and met Michael asleep in front of the door, beside his half bottle of whiskey. His father yelled but Michael didn't move. His mother tapped him. 'Michael? Michael!'

Michael opened his eyes.

His father sighed and said, 'He is alive,' and inserted the key into the door. He dropped his books on the table in the centre of the living room and sank onto one of the silver coloured sofas. The woman helped her son into the house to the dining room where the two of them sat.

'Michael, what are you doing to yourself,' his father asked.

Michael felt sick from the whisky he had. 'I wanted to travel. I am back and will move out as soon as I find a place,' he replied.

'Do you know what you put us through?' his mother asked. 'It took the police two weeks to tell us you had left Sydney. We thought you were in New Zealand. The New Zealand police had no record of your whereabouts either. I became distressed when we heard you were in Nigeria.'

'What did you go to do in Nigeria, Michael?' his father asked. 'Who do you know there? Your mother kept calling her cousins she last spoke to seven years ago to ask for you. A cunning cousin of hers even demanded some money to help in the search.'

'Dad, I am thirty-three. There's nothing wrong if I want to travel around. Why were you not worried while I was living in New Zealand?'

'New Zealand is a safe place. What are you talking about? You have a country here. A very good country with a promising future for you as a citizen, and you chase a country of our past. Do you think if Nigeria was better than Australia, your mother and I would be here?'

'Are you still into that homosexual lifestyle, Michael?' his mother asked.

Michael looked over the table.

'We will discuss that later,' said his father. 'Go and have a shower, Michael. Your mother will make something for you to eat.'

Michael left the living room and his mother followed.

His father lifted one of the books he brought home and opened the first page when he heard Michael's angry voice from the bedroom. Michael came out in a rage.

'What's the problem,' his father asked.

'The problem is you and your mad wife,' he answered.

His mother walked into the living room.

Michael kicked one of the dining chairs and it hit the wall. He then walked out of the house.

'Michael,' his father shouted. 'Who do you think you are? Where do you think you are going?'

'To hell!' Michael yelled.

'What did you say to him,' his father asked his mother.

He passed the public library and found his way to Hornsby train station. He jumped over a turnstile and almost tripped over. No one stopped him. He passed by some high school girls and an elderly man, who sat on a wooden bench, staring at him. People sat on similar benches waiting for the next train. He didn't stop running. He jumped onto the tracks. A train approached. Some of school kids screamed. The oncoming train whistled and hurried violently like a gymnastic bull. It was travelling through Normanhurst, Thornleigh, Pennant Hill, right up to Chestwood, and Michael vanished under its belly.

ACKNOWLEDGEMENT

This work would not have been possible without the reliable and generous support of my mentor, James George. His advice and astute suggestions have drastically improved my approach to writing.

I will like to thank my family, friends and colleagues who supported me throughout the year I wrote this work; most especially my wife, Tega, who was my fiancée at the time. She made me believe even when hope appeared pale. My heartfelt thanks also go to Angela Bradley and Late Des Mann, who kept reassuring me. And to Su'eddie Agema, I salute. He wanted this work to see the light of the day.

Lastly, I will like to thank Terver Asongo, Elizabeth Ardley, Gary Ferguson and Angelina Sbroma for their editing and feedback.

MYLES OJABO

www.ingramcontent.com/pod-product-compliance
Lightning Source LLC
Chambersburg PA
CBHW032305070726
47590CB00015B/536

* 9 7 8 0 4 7 3 4 1 1 7 7 0 *